Bridge to Bridge

Hamid Nakhostin Ahmadi

Volume 1

Contents

Introduction

What you are about to read is not merely a book—it is a chronicle of a dream, a journey woven from countless threads of perseverance, hope, and the sheer will to succeed. This is the story of my arrival on American soil—a tale shared by many new immigrants who leave behind familiar lands in search of a new beginning, yet it is also uniquely my own.

From the moment I set foot in the United States, every day was a lesson in courage and resilience. I arrived with little more than a heart full of ambition and a spirit determined to overcome every obstacle. The early days were a whirlwind of challenges: learning a new language, understanding an unfamiliar culture, and adjusting to a society where every small step forward required immense effort. I embraced every hardship, knowing that each struggle was a stepping stone toward my envisioned life.

My journey was not paved with immediate success or comfort. I undertook a series of jobs that many might overlook—a carpet mover, a dishwasher in a busy restaurant, a salesman in the competitive world of automobiles. With each role, I learned the value of hard work, the importance of persistence, and the strength that lies within when one refuses to give up. These humble beginnings were, in fact, my training ground. They prepared me to face future challenges, instilling in me an unyielding belief that no matter how many times I was knocked down, I had the power to rise again.

Every job, every challenge, and every small victory added layers to my character. The difficulties of mastering a new language and assimilating into an unfamiliar culture tested my limits, but they also revealed to me the vast reservoir of strength that lay dormant within. I understood that an immigrant's journey is one of constant reinvention—a cycle of learning, adapting, and ultimately, triumphing over adversity.

Perhaps one of the most profound challenges was the separation from my family—a painful reminder of the sacrifices made in pursuit of a better life. The physical distance from loved ones often deepened the sense of isolation, yet it also taught me the importance of forging new bonds and finding support in unexpected places. In the midst of these trials, fate introduced me to a beacon of light: my wife. Her unwavering support, compassion, and love transformed my struggles into a shared mission. With her by my side, I discovered not only a partner in life but also a renewed purpose that fueled my determination to succeed.

It is with a heart overflowing with gratitude that I dedicate this book to the people who have been my pillars of strength. To my beloved wife, Zohreh, whose boundless encouragement and steadfast belief in my dreams have been my guiding light during the darkest moments—this work is a testament to your love and resilience. And to my sons, Kayvone (Kevin) and Kayhan, who inspire me every day with their innocence and courage, and who I love more than life itself. Your smiles and faith in our future have been the very fuel that propelled me forward, reminding me that every sacrifice made was for the promise of a brighter tomorrow.

This book is more than a memoir; it is a tribute to the spirit of every immigrant who dares to dream in the face of overwhelming odds. It is an invitation to journey with me through the valleys of hardship and the peaks of triumph, to experience the bittersweet symphony of struggle and success. As you turn these pages, may you find not just a story, but a message of hope—a reminder that no matter where you come from, the promise of a new beginning is always within reach.

Chapter 1:
Iran Before the Revolution

Before 1978, Iran was a land of striking contrasts, a place where the ancient and the modern collided in ways that could both inspire and unsettle. It was a country on the cusp of transformation, a nation where towering skyscrapers overshadowed centuries-old bazaars and where sleek, imported cars zipped through streets lined with ornate mosques. On the surface, Iran radiated progress and prosperity, a vision of a nation rising confidently into the future. Yet, beneath this polished exterior, a cauldron of discontent simmered, fueled by a collision of ideologies, values, and suppressed voices.

A Country of Contrasts

To walk through Tehran in the 1970s was to step into a mosaic of paradoxes. The city itself was a marvel, a bustling metropolis that sought to emulate the modernity of Western capitals like Paris and New York. Glittering department stores advertised the latest European fashions, while neon signs glowed with the names of foreign brands, signaling Iran's embrace of global consumerism. Cafés and cinemas drew the urban elite, who sat sipping espresso or watching the latest Hollywood blockbusters, their conversations peppered with French or English phrases.

But a few streets away, the heart of traditional Tehran pulsed with a different rhythm. In the grand bazaar, the air was thick with the aroma of saffron, cardamom, and fresh-baked flatbread. Merchants haggled loudly over the price of silk, copperware, or Persian carpets, their stalls stacked high with goods that carried the weight of centuries of craftsmanship. Here, the cadence of life was slower, steeped in customs that had endured through countless dynasties. It was a world that resisted the pull of modernity, holding fast to traditions that seemed immovable.

This duality extended far beyond the capital. In the southern city of Shiraz, the gardens of Eram offered a serene escape, their fountains, and cypress trees evoking the poetry of Hafez. Isfahan dazzled with its turquoise domes and majestic bridges, a testament to Iran's architectural genius. Meanwhile, in Abadan, the hum of oil refineries underscored the industrial aspirations of a nation determined to assert itself on the global stage.

Yet, these contrasts were more than just aesthetic. They were reflective of a deeper societal tension. The Iran of the 1970s was a nation caught between two worlds: one that looked to the West for inspiration and progress and another that sought solace in its rich Persian heritage and Islamic traditions.

The Shah's Grand Vision

At the center of this evolving landscape stood Mohammad Reza Shah Pahlavi, a ruler with grand ambitions. To his supporters, the Shah was a visionary, a leader determined to drag Iran into the modern age. Under his rule, the country embarked on sweeping reforms as part of the White Revolution—a series of initiatives aimed at industrializing the economy, redistributing land to peasants, and promoting education and women's rights.

In many ways, the Shah's vision was transformative. Roads and railways crisscrossed the nation, connecting once-isolated villages to the burgeoning cities. Universities expanded, and students poured into classrooms that promised them a brighter future. The oil boom of the 1970s flooded the country with wealth, funding projects that dazzled the world—a modern healthcare system, state-of-the-art infrastructure, and a military that rivaled the most powerful nations.

Yet, for all its promise, the Shah's vision came at a cost. His relentless drive for modernization often felt imposed, leaving many Iranians feeling alienated from the changes sweeping through their lives. The land reforms, though intended to empower peasants, disrupted traditional agricultural practices and displaced thousands of rural families. The urbanization that the Shah championed brought with it a widening gap between the rich and the poor, as luxury high-rises sprouted in cities while many lived in shantytowns on the outskirts.

The Shah's vision for Iran was grand, rooted in the ideals of modernization, secularization, and alignment with Western powers. He dreamed of transforming the country into a global economic and cultural powerhouse, a modern empire worthy of its ancient lineage.

Farmers, promised prosperity through land reforms, often found themselves struggling to make ends meet on plots too small to sustain their families. Traditional landowners, stripped of their influence, harbored resentment toward a government they viewed as reckless and heavy-handed. Religious leaders, too, saw the Shah's secular policies as an affront to Islamic values, an attack on the moral and cultural fabric of the nation.

Meanwhile, rapid industrialization left many feeling disoriented. Factories and machinery appeared overnight, but the speed of change often outpaced the people's ability to adapt. Rural communities, steeped in centuries-old traditions, were thrust into a foreign and soulless modernity. And for all the Shah's promises, the wealth generated by the oil boom seemed to pool in the hands of the elite, leaving a wide gap between the privileged few and the struggling majority.

The Hidden Tensions

Beneath the veneer of progress, Iran was a country simmering with discontent. The Shah's regime was authoritarian, brooking no dissent. The secret police, SAVAK, operated with ruthless efficiency, silencing critics and instilling a climate of fear. Political freedoms were curtailed, and opposition parties were either banned or rendered impotent. Intellectuals, students, and clerics who dared to challenge the regime often found themselves imprisoned—or worse.

But repression alone couldn't stifle the growing discontent. The rapid pace of modernization left many feeling unmoored, their identities caught between tradition and progress. In the countryside, the disruption of agrarian life bred resentment, as villagers saw their livelihoods vanish in the name of development. In the cities, the Westernized elite drew the ire of those who felt excluded from the benefits of modernization. The cultural shifts—women in miniskirts, men in sharp suits, the growing presence of Western media—clashed with the values of a deeply religious society, fueling a sense of moral and cultural alienation.

For the older generation, the changes often felt like an assault on Iran's soul. They mourned the erosion of traditions and the displacement of Persian poetry and music by foreign films and disco. For the younger generation, particularly the university students, the discontent took a different form. They questioned the Shah's ties to the West, particularly to the United States, seeing his regime as a puppet of foreign powers. They longed for a nation that was not just modern but truly independent, free from the influence of imperialists.

The Seeds of Revolution

Amidst this growing unrest, a new voice began to emerge—one that would eventually rally the discontented masses. Ayatollah Ruhollah Khomeini, exiled in Najaf, Iraq, was a cleric who spoke to the frustrations of a population that felt overlooked and oppressed. From his distant sanctuary, Khomeini's fiery sermons circulated in secret, denouncing the Shah as a tyrant and calling for an Islamic government that would restore the moral and spiritual foundation of Iran.

Khomeini's words resonated deeply, particularly with the working class and the rural poor, who saw in his message a return to the values that modernization seemed to have trampled. His call for justice and equity struck a chord in a country where wealth and power were increasingly concentrated in the hands of a few.

At the same time, the intellectuals and students who once dreamed of a secular, democratic Iran found themselves disillusioned with the Shah's empty promises. They joined forces with the clerics, their shared frustration forming an unlikely coalition of traditionalists and progressives.

My World Before It Changed

In 1978, I was a young man, just beginning to understand the complexities of the world around me. I grew up surrounded by the vibrant contradictions of Iranian society, learning to navigate the divide between my family's traditions and the modern influences creeping into our lives. My parents believed in education, ambition, and the promise of a better future. They wanted me to thrive in a world that seemed to be changing faster than anyone could fully grasp.

Yet, even as I pursued my studies and dreamed of a future that seemed boundless, I couldn't ignore the unease that hung in the air. The conversations at family gatherings turned increasingly political, the optimism of the older generation giving way to murmurs of dissatisfaction. Friends and relatives whispered about the arrests, the corruption, the cracks forming in the foundation of the Shah's regime.

Life in pre-revolution Iran was a mix of beauty and tension. The streets of Tehran offered dazzling sights and sounds, but the undercurrent of unease was always present, like a storm gathering on the horizon. It was a time of possibility, yes, but also of uncertainty—a nation poised on the edge of transformation, waiting for the moment when everything would change.

The Allure of Modernity

To walk through the streets of Tehran in the 1970s was to step into a dazzling world that seemed to promise limitless possibilities. The city pulsed with an infectious energy, a blend of ancient Persian culture and the intoxicating allure of Western modernity. There were signs of transformation everywhere you looked—gleaming storefronts, bustling avenues, and a population eager to embrace the future.

A City on the Rise

Tehran, the beating heart of Iran, was evolving at an astonishing pace. Wide boulevards such as Pahlavi Street (now Vali Asr) were lined with luxury boutiques that showcased the finest goods from Europe and beyond. French perfumes, Italian leather shoes, and Swiss watches sat behind polished glass displays, enticing passersby with their elegance. Shopping was not just a necessity—it was an event, a statement of status and aspiration. Women in chic miniskirts and bell-bottom trousers browsed the latest fashion trends, their confidence mirrored in their brightly painted nails and meticulously coiffed hair. Men in tailored suits, their ties perfectly knotted, strode purposefully through the city, their polished shoes clicking against the pavement.

At night, the city transformed into a playground of lights and music. Neon signs illuminated the skyline, announcing the names of popular restaurants, nightclubs, and cinemas. Nightlife thrived, especially in northern Tehran, where the elite gathered to sip cocktails and dance under glittering chandeliers in opulent clubs. The chatter of voices and the rhythmic beats of live bands filled the air, creating an atmosphere that was both glamorous and carefree.

The Soundtrack of Change

The music of the era captured the essence of this cultural shift, providing a soundtrack to a society in flux. Pop stars like Googoosh, Dariush, and Ebi rose to stardom, their voices blending the soul of Persian tradition with the vibrancy of Western influence. Googoosh, with her striking beauty and magnetic stage presence, was the face of a new, modern Iran. Her songs resonated with the youth, her lyrics touching on themes of love, longing, and rebellion. Dariush's poignant ballads and Ebi's charismatic performances added depth to a music scene that was as dynamic as the country itself.

Their music poured out of cafes, cars, and family gatherings, a unifying force that brought people together. Radios played their hits on repeat, while record stores reported brisk sales of vinyl albums adorned with bold, colorful artwork. For many, these songs weren't just entertainment—they were an anthem of a generation caught between the old and the new.

Television and cinema played an equally transformative role. Domestic films began to explore the nuances of Iranian society, offering both escapism and introspection. Audiences flocked to theaters, where the latest Hollywood blockbusters played alongside Iranian films that tackled themes of identity, class, and change. Actors and actresses became household names, their faces adorning glossy magazines that flew off newsstands.

Economic Prosperity and Aspirations

Beneath the cultural renaissance lay an economic boom that fueled Iran's rapid modernization. The oil boom of the 1970s brought unprecedented wealth to the country, and the government, under the Shah's leadership, poured resources into ambitious infrastructure projects. Highways and roads stretched across the nation, connecting remote villages to bustling cities. Airports expanded, their gleaming terminals a testament to the nation's aspirations for global prominence. Modern apartment buildings and office towers rose alongside traditional brick homes, reshaping the skyline.

The middle class flourished during this time. Families who once lived modestly now enjoyed the trappings of a rising standard of living. New appliances—televisions, refrigerators, and washing machines—filled homes, symbols of progress and prosperity. Cars became increasingly common, and traffic jams in Tehran were both a frustration and a sign of success.

Education was a cornerstone of this progress. Schools and universities expanded to accommodate a surge of students, many of whom were the first in their families to pursue higher education. Young men and women studied fields ranging from engineering to literature, their dreams fueled by the belief that they could contribute to Iran's bright future. Healthcare, too, saw significant improvements, with modern hospitals and clinics springing up in both urban and rural areas.

A Dream Wrapped in Glamor

To many, life in Tehran during this era seemed like a dream come true. On weekends, families flocked to the city's parks for picnics, spreading colorful carpets under the shade of trees. They shared plates of kebab, fresh herbs, and warm flatbread, their laughter filling the air. Young couples strolled along the paths, their eyes filled with hope for a future that seemed as boundless as the sky.

The allure of modernity was undeniable. It was in the clinking of glasses at lavish parties, the hum of brand-new refrigerators in middle-class homes, and the sparkle of sequined dresses worn to nightclubs. It was in the way Tehran's skyline reached higher and higher, each building a testament to the belief that Iran could stand shoulder to shoulder with the great nations of the world.

The Undercurrent of Unease

But beneath this veneer of progress, cracks began to form. While the middle class and elite basked in the glow of modernity, many others felt left behind. In rural areas, the rapid pace of change seemed alien and invasive, disrupting traditional ways of life. For every skyscraper built in Tehran, there were countless villages that still lacked basic infrastructure. The stark contrast between the haves and have-nots became a growing source of tension, feeding a quiet resentment that would soon erupt into the open.

The cultural shifts, too, were not without controversy. To some, the miniskirts and bell-bottoms, the Western pop music, and the Hollywood films felt like an erosion of Iran's identity, a betrayal of its rich heritage and Islamic values. For every woman who embraced the latest fashion trends, there were others who clung to their chadors, feeling increasingly out of place in a society that seemed to prioritize Western ideals over Persian traditions.

Tehran, for all its glamour and progress, was a microcosm of a nation divided. It represented both the pinnacle of what Iran could achieve and the deep fractures that modernization had wrought. The allure of modernity was powerful, but it came with a price—a price that many were unwilling to pay. As the 1970s drew to a close, the vibrant streets of Tehran would soon give way to protests, their cries for justice and change echoing through the city that had once seemed unstoppable.

The Shadows of Authoritarianism

Beneath the glittering façade of progress and modernity that defined Iran in the 1970s lay an oppressive undercurrent that few dared to challenge openly. The government of Mohammad Reza Pahlavi, the Shah, was lauded by Western powers for its ambitious modernization programs, yet it was simultaneously a regime that stifled freedom, crushed dissent, and ruled with an iron fist. While skyscrapers rose and highways sprawled, the spirit of the Iranian people was often shackled by fear and silence.

Universities as Hotbeds of Resistance

Despite the pervasive control, resistance simmered beneath the surface, especially in universities. Campuses became the epicenters of political awareness, places where students debated the future of their country and dared to dream of a freer, fairer Iran. Posters with subversive slogans appeared on walls overnight, and pamphlets criticizing the Shah circulated discreetly among students. Study groups doubled as planning cells, where strategies for protests were discussed in whispers.

When protests erupted, they were met with swift and brutal retaliation. SAVAK agents infiltrated the student movements, identifying leaders who were later arrested or disappeared. Demonstrations were broken up with tear gas, batons, and gunfire. Images of bloodied students and grieving parents became a stark counterpoint to the glossy propaganda touting Iran's progress. Each crackdown only deepened the divide between the regime and the people, fueling the anger that would one day boil over.

The Disconnect Grows

The Shah's heavy-handed rule created a chasm between the government and its citizens. In lavish palaces, the royal court hosted extravagant banquets, attended by foreign dignitaries and glittering with jewels and luxury. Meanwhile, in the streets, ordinary Iranians grappled with inflation, unemployment, and a sense of alienation. The regime's obsession with Westernization often felt dismissive of the country's deep-rooted traditions and values, further alienating large swathes of the population.

The Shah's reliance on foreign powers, particularly the United States, was another sore point. To many Iranians, the regime seemed less like a sovereign government and more like a puppet of Western interests. The sight of American advisors and businesses dominating sectors of the economy only reinforced the perception that Iran's wealth and independence were being compromised. This sentiment found its voice in the rhetoric of opposition leaders, who decried the Shah as a betrayer of Iran's heritage and sovereignty.

A Ticking Time Bomb

By the late 1970s, the cracks in the Shah's carefully constructed façade of progress were impossible to ignore. The glittering towers of Tehran cast long shadows over a nation growing restless and disillusioned. The glamour of modernity could no longer mask the deep inequalities, the stifled voices, and the pervasive fear. Every act of repression, every whisper of dissent, added fuel to the growing fire of resistance.

The streets of Tehran, once bustling with the sounds of commerce and celebration, began to echo with the chants of protestors. "Death to the Shah!" became the rallying cry of a people who had reached their breaking point. For decades, the regime had suppressed these voices, but now, they were rising in unison, demanding change. The Shah's vision of a modern Iran had turned into a nightmare for many, and the shadows of authoritarianism were about to give way to the blinding light of revolution.

The Struggle of Identity

In the midst of Iran's rapid transformation during the Shah's reign, the country found itself grappling with an existential crisis—a battle between modernity and tradition, between progress and heritage. The Shah's aggressive push for Westernization, though celebrated in certain circles, sowed seeds of alienation and unrest among vast segments of society. The struggle to define what it meant to be Iranian in this evolving landscape became a source of tension, leaving deep cultural and social scars.

Urban Modernity vs. Rural Tradition

In the cities, the march toward Western-style modernity was impossible to ignore. Men and women in tailored suits and designer dresses populated Tehran's bustling streets. Billboards advertised the latest European fashions, American films dominated cinema screens, and cafes buzzed with chatter over cappuccinos and imported cigarettes. The urban elite reveled in this newfound cosmopolitanism, viewing it as a marker of progress, a way to place Iran on the global stage.

But as the cities soared into this Westernized future, the countryside was left behind, both materially and culturally. In rural areas, where agriculture and age-old traditions still defined daily life, the rapid modernization felt like an invasion. Women clad in miniskirts and men adopting Western hairstyles were symbols of a culture slipping away from its roots. Traditional families looked on with unease as their children, influenced by city life, began questioning age-old customs. Many rural Iranians found themselves asking: *What does it mean to be Iranian in a world where our traditions are being cast aside?*

Economic inequality only heightened these feelings of alienation. The oil boom of the 1970s had poured unprecedented wealth into the country, but much of it remained concentrated in the hands of the urban elite. Roads and factories might have sprung up in some rural areas, but the benefits were unevenly distributed. Farmers, who had once been promised prosperity under the Shah's land reforms, often found themselves worse off, their small plots unable to compete with large agricultural enterprises. The glittering

skyscrapers of Tehran became symbols of a widening chasm—
a gap not just of wealth, but of culture and identity.

The Role of Religion and the Rise of Khomeini

In this vacuum of alienation, religious leaders stepped in to fill the void, offering a counter-narrative to the Shah's vision. Among them, Ayatollah Ruhollah Khomeini emerged as a powerful voice of opposition. Forced into exile after publicly denouncing the Shah in the early 1960s, Khomeini became the spiritual leader of a growing resistance movement. From the safety of exile in Najaf, Iraq, and later in Paris, he delivered speeches and writings that condemned the Shah's regime as morally bankrupt and un-Islamic.

Khomeini's message resonated deeply with those who felt excluded from Iran's rapid modernization. His words spoke to the rural poor, who saw their way of life slipping away under the weight of industrialization. They spoke to the religiously devout, who viewed the Shah's secular policies—such as granting women the right to vote and banning the hijab in public institutions—as direct attacks on their faith and identity. They also spoke to the disillusioned youth, whose idealism had been crushed by the corruption and authoritarianism of the government.

Khomeini's rhetoric was more than just criticism; it was a promise of redemption. He envisioned an Iran that returned to its Islamic roots, where justice, equality, and morality would replace the excesses and inequities of the Shah's rule. For those who felt adrift in a rapidly changing world, his vision offered an anchor, a sense of purpose and belonging.

The Cultural Schism

This struggle of identity was not merely a conflict between modernity and tradition; it was a deeply personal battle for many Iranians. Families found themselves divided along generational and ideological lines. In urban homes, younger siblings clad in bell-bottom jeans and rock band T-shirts clashed with elder relatives who clung to traditional Persian values. Conversations around dinner tables turned into heated debates over what Iran should become. Should the country embrace its ancient heritage, or should it continue down the path of Westernization?

The schism also played out in public spaces. Women who chose to wear the chador—the traditional Islamic covering—were increasingly viewed with suspicion or even ridicule in the cities. Conversely, those who dressed in Western fashion were scorned in conservative rural communities. This divide created an atmosphere of mutual distrust, where neither side felt fully accepted or understood.

Propaganda and Resistance

The Shah's regime attempted to address this identity crisis through a barrage of state-sponsored propaganda. Television programs celebrated Iran's ancient Persian history while simultaneously glorifying its modern advancements. Public speeches extolled the virtues of progress and positioned the Shah as the ultimate guardian of the nation's future. Yet these efforts often rang hollow to those who felt excluded or oppressed by the very system that claimed to represent them.

Khomeini's counter-movement was no less strategic. From exile, he relied on a network of loyal clerics and underground activists to distribute his sermons and writings. Tapes of his speeches were smuggled into Iran and copied en masse, passed from hand to hand in mosques, bazaars, and private homes. These messages painted the Shah as a tyrant beholden to Western interests and called on Iranians to reclaim their country and identity through Islamic values. For many, these recordings were more than just words; they were a lifeline, a call to action in a time of profound uncertainty.

A Nation on the Brink

By the late 1970s, the struggle for identity had reached a boiling point. In the countryside, farmers who had once hoped for prosperity under the Shah's reforms now looked to religious leaders for answers. In the cities, students and intellectuals, disillusioned with the promises of modernization, began questioning whether Westernization had come at too high a cost. Even within the Shah's own circle, whispers of doubt began to emerge, as it became clear that the regime's vision for Iran was increasingly at odds with the desires of its people.

The struggle was no longer confined to ideology; it was now a fight for the soul of the nation. Would Iran continue its march toward Western-style modernity, or would it return to its Islamic and Persian roots? The answer would soon erupt in the streets, as the simmering tensions of identity, culture, and power gave way to revolution. In the end, the battle for Iran's future would not just reshape the country—it would redefine what it meant to be Iranian in a world torn between tradition and change.

A Glimpse of Everyday Life

Amid the simmering political tensions and looming revolution, daily life in Iran held a rhythm that, for many, felt remarkably vibrant and free. The country was a mosaic of experiences, a tapestry woven with moments of joy, cultural richness, and a freedom of choice that allowed individuals to define their lives on their terms. It was a time when the cracks in society were visible but not yet deep enough to overshadow the beauty and promise of ordinary existence.

The Freedom of Choice

In this era, the streets of Tehran, Isfahan, and Shiraz were alive with a spectrum of colors and styles that reflected the choices available to Iranians. Women strolled confidently, some dressed in miniskirts and bold hairstyles that mirrored the latest trends in Paris and London, while others opted for the flowing chadors and modesty rooted in Persian tradition. There was no single standard; instead, the streets became a catwalk of individuality and expression. Men wore tailored suits, leather jackets, or traditional tunics, embodying a blend of old and new that defined the country's evolving identity.

For young people like me, this duality was exhilarating. We could step into a world that allowed us to explore global influences while remaining deeply rooted in the traditions of our ancestors. My sisters could wear jeans and listen to pop music one day, then don silk scarves to join my grandmother at the mosque the next. This coexistence of tradition and modernity created an atmosphere where life felt expansive, as though anything was possible.

The Vibrant Pulse of Public Spaces

Public spaces were the heart of Iranian life. Parks, especially on weekends, teemed with families who carried heavy baskets filled with steaming rice, grilled kebabs, and fragrant stews. The smell of saffron and freshly baked bread lingered in the air as children played games and parents lounged on rugs, sipping hot tea from delicate glasses. These gatherings were more than just leisure; they were a celebration of community, a reminder of the importance of connection in a rapidly changing world.

The bazaars were equally dynamic. Rows upon rows of stalls overflowed with goods—plump tomatoes, fragrant spices, handwoven carpets, and glittering jewelry. The hum of bargaining voices and the clinking of coins created a symphony unique to these spaces. Vendors would invite passersby with hearty calls, offering samples of everything from candied nuts to saffron-infused sweets. The bazaars weren't just places to shop; they were theaters of social interaction, where everyone from housewives to businessmen came to exchange not only goods but stories, gossip, and laughter.

Cafés, meanwhile, provided a different kind of refuge. These spaces were the breeding grounds for ideas, where intellectuals, artists, and students gathered to debate the latest books, political theories, and cultural trends. The conversations flowed as freely as the tea, blending the wisdom of Persian poetry with the allure of Western philosophy. In one corner, you might find a heated discussion about Rumi's verses, while at the next table, someone might passionately argue about Sartre or Nietzsche. These discussions shaped a generation, leaving young minds like mine filled with dreams of blending our heritage with the promise of modernity.

Dreams of Greatness

Despite the political undercurrents, there was a pervasive optimism among many young Iranians. We believed that our country was on the cusp of something extraordinary. Iran's rich heritage, its thriving arts, and its growing economy seemed to promise a future where modernity and tradition could coexist harmoniously. We didn't see ourselves as having to choose between the two; rather, we imagined a synthesis that honored both.

My friends and I often spent hours envisioning this future. We saw ourselves as architects of a society that could take pride in its Persian roots while embracing the innovations of the modern world. Whether we were discussing philosophy in cafés, performing music, or simply walking through the bustling streets of Tehran, there was an undercurrent of excitement. We were part of a generation that believed in possibility, in the idea that Iran's future could be as vibrant and multifaceted as its present.

A Fragile Paradise

Yet, even in these moments of joy and optimism, there was an unspoken awareness of the fragility of it all. We lived in a world of contrasts—where the freedom to choose how to live, what to wear, and what to dream existed alongside the silent but pervasive presence of an authoritarian regime. While we picnicked in parks and played music in concert halls, whispers of dissent and discontent were beginning to ripple through society.

For many of us, these whispers felt distant, almost unreal. The laughter in the bazaars, the debates in the cafés, the music at concerts—all of it felt too vibrant, too alive, to be threatened. Yet, in hindsight, these moments were the last flickers of a golden age, a fleeting glimpse of what Iran could have been before the storm of revolution swept it all away. The joy and freedom we experienced were real, but they existed on borrowed time, suspended in a delicate balance that could not last.

The Illusion of Stability

In hindsight, the optimism we felt in those days was a delicate bubble, floating precariously in a storm. The laughter in the bazaars, the debates in cafés, and the music that filled our homes gave the impression of a nation in harmony, but this harmony was an illusion, carefully curated by the Shah's regime. We believed in the stability of the world around us because we wanted to believe—because the alternative was too unsettling to consider.

A Fragile Facade

The Shah's vision of progress was dazzling on the surface. Tehran's glittering avenues, dotted with luxury boutiques and skyscrapers, seemed to whisper promises of a bright future. The oil boom of the 1970s had fueled rapid economic growth, and the government's investment in infrastructure painted a picture of advancement. Yet beneath this veneer lay cracks too deep to ignore, even if many of us tried.

Economic inequality was one of the most glaring fissures. While the urban elite dined in upscale restaurants and sent their children to Western universities, millions in rural areas struggled to feed their families. For every family enjoying a weekend picnic in a lush park, there were countless others toiling in poverty, their lives untouched by the supposed prosperity of the Shah's modern Iran. The divide between the haves and the have-nots wasn't just economic; it was cultural. The rural poor and the religiously conservative felt alienated by the rapid Westernization that the Shah championed. They saw a government that celebrated miniskirts and jazz clubs while neglecting the values and traditions that had defined their lives for generations.

A Society on Edge

As young people, we lived our lives on the surface of this fragile stability, largely oblivious to the deeper unrest. For us, the world was a stage, and we were eager players, performing music, dreaming of futures, and imagining a society that could blend the best of East and West. But whispers of dissent began to creep into the edges of our lives. Friends spoke cautiously of protests at universities, of classmates who had disappeared after being too vocal in their criticism of the regime. SAVAK, the Shah's secret police, was a shadowy presence that rarely touched our immediate circle but always loomed in the periphery.

Even in our most carefree moments, there was a sense of something unspoken, an awareness that the freedoms we enjoyed came at a cost. We didn't talk about politics openly, even among close friends. To do so felt risky, as though voicing dissatisfaction might summon the very forces that would destroy the world we cherished. This silence was its own form of complicity, a tacit agreement to ignore the storm clouds gathering on the horizon.

The Unraveling

When the revolution began in 1978, it felt distant at first, like the echo of a drumbeat from another world. We watched from the sidelines, confident that the Shah's regime, with its wealth, power, and Western allies, would weather the storm. But as the protests grew larger and more relentless, it became impossible to ignore the cracks widening beneath our feet. The streets we had walked so confidently, the parks where families picnicked, the cafés where intellectuals debated—all of it began to change. The laughter faded, replaced by the chants of protesters and the heavy presence of soldiers.

The revolution swept through the country like a tidal wave, erasing everything in its path. It wasn't just the monarchy that fell—it was the entire way of life we had known. The vibrant cultural scene, the sense of social freedom, and the belief in progress vanished almost overnight. By 1979, the Iran we had grown up in was unrecognizable.

The Loss of Freedom

The changes were swift and absolute. Women, who had once strolled freely in miniskirts or traditional garb, were now forced to wear the hijab. Music, once the soul of our generation, was silenced under the weight of censorship. Songs that had filled the air with hope and passion were replaced by solemn chants of revolution or banned entirely. Cinemas that had showcased the latest Hollywood films and Iranian masterpieces closed their doors or restricted their screens to approved propaganda. The once-lively cafés became quiet, their tables no longer hosting debates on art and philosophy but instead hushed whispers of fear and loss.

The transformation was suffocating, not just for those who remained but also for those of us who had left. For me, the Iran of my youth became a memory frozen in time, untouched by the realities of the new regime. It was a place of vibrant bazaars, late-night music sessions, and dreams of a bright future—a vision that now felt like a cruel mirage.

Bittersweet Memories

For those of us who left before the revolution, the Iran we carry in our hearts is a bittersweet memory. It is a land of dazzling contradictions, where modernity and tradition coexisted in an uneasy but beautiful balance. We remember the parks, the music, the optimism of youth—but these memories are haunted by the knowledge of what came after. We mourn not just the loss of a homeland but the loss of a possibility, of a future where Iran might have navigated its challenges without losing its soul.

Even now, decades later, I sometimes dream of that time. In my dreams, the streets of Tehran are alive with music and laughter, the parks filled with families, the cafés buzzing with debate. For a moment, I feel the warmth of that world again, the promise and the hope. But then I wake, and the dream dissolves, leaving behind the shadow of a revolution that changed everything.

A Testament to What Was

The stories of those days remain a testament to what Iran once was—and what it could have been. They are reminders of a vibrant, hopeful era that was lost to the tides of history. For me, and for so many others, these memories are both a comfort and a sorrow, a glimpse of a golden age that will forever live in the shadow of what came after.

Chapter 2:
The Drama of Departure

By the middle of 1978, Iran had become a nation standing on a precipice, its fate teetering between upheaval and collapse. The air was thick with unease, an invisible force that settled into the daily lives of every citizen. The streets of Tehran, once symbols of progress and vitality, had become battlegrounds. Protesters chanted slogans of defiance against the Shah's regime, their voices cutting through the chaos of tear gas and the heavy boots of riot police. The vibrant hum of modern life—the laughter in cafés, the music spilling from shopfronts, the chatter of bustling bazaars—was slowly being drowned out by the drumbeat of revolution.

The End of Normalcy

For young people like me, the chaos unfolding outside was a paradox: impossible to ignore, yet strangely surreal. We watched the world we knew unravel in slow motion. Friends and neighbors disappeared into the void, some fleeing abroad while others were swallowed by the shadowy grip of the regime. Fear became a constant undercurrent, an uninvited guest at every family gathering. Yet, even as the foundations of society crumbled, we clung to a fragile semblance of normalcy.

My days were filled with music, studies, and stolen moments of joy with friends. We laughed, debated, and dreamed as if our shared optimism could hold the encroaching darkness at bay. But beneath the surface, there was an unspoken understanding: our time was running out. The world we had grown up in—the vibrant, hopeful Iran of our youth—was slipping away, and there was no way to stop it.

A Life-Changing Visit

That summer, when my aunt Shahla returned to Iran after four years in the United States, it was as if she had brought another world with her. From the moment she stepped off the plane, her presence radiated something foreign yet magnetic. Dressed in crisp Western clothing, her demeanor exuded a confidence and ease that seemed untouched by the turmoil gripping Iran.

Shahla's visit was a rare bright spot during an otherwise dark and uncertain time. To me, she was a walking symbol of possibility—a testament to a life beyond the confines of Iran's political unrest and cultural constraints. Her stories, shared over endless cups of tea and lively family dinners, were nothing short of transformative.

A Glimpse of Another World

Around the dinner table, her voice painted pictures of vibrant American cities teeming with life. She spoke of bustling streets lined with towering skyscrapers, of universities brimming with resources and opportunities, and of a society where personal freedom was not just an abstract ideal but a daily reality.

"Imagine walking into a library and finding entire floors of books on anything you could ever want to learn," she said one evening, her eyes lighting up with excitement. "Or walking into a store and finding every fruit, every vegetable, no matter the season!"

Her descriptions were spellbinding. She told us about her life in Los Angeles, where she and Ray had built a home filled with warmth and love, where weekends were spent exploring beaches or attending music festivals, and where people from all walks of life seemed to coexist in a way that felt impossible in Iran.

For a young man trapped between the suffocating grip of political unrest and the dreams he held for a brighter future, her words were intoxicating. Her stories weren't just about material abundance or conveniences—they were about possibility, about carving out a life defined by choice rather than circumstance.

The Suggestion That Changed Everything

One afternoon, as the summer sun streamed through the windows of our family's living room, Shahla and I found ourselves in a quiet conversation. She had been asking about my studies, my aspirations, and what I imagined my future might look like.

"Why don't you come to America and continue your education?" she said, her voice warm and matter-of-fact, as though the suggestion were as simple as asking me to join her for tea.

Her words landed like an earthquake. I froze, unsure if I'd heard her correctly. America? Me? The thought of leaving Iran, of venturing halfway across the world, had always felt like a dream so distant it was hardly worth entertaining.

"But... how?" I stammered, my mind racing with questions. How would I afford it? How could I leave my family behind? What if I failed?

She smiled, a knowing look in her eyes. "You're smart, ambitious, and hardworking. There are scholarships, community colleges, and ways to make it work. Ray and I can help you get started. You just need to take the first step."

Her words planted a seed, and though it was small at first, it began to grow with a ferocity I hadn't expected. For the first time, the idea of studying in the United States felt like more than just an unattainable fantasy—it felt possible.

The Weight of Possibility

That night, as I lay in bed, her words echoed in my mind. My thoughts swung wildly between exhilaration and doubt. Could I really do it? Could I leave my family, my friends, and everything I knew behind? Would I fit into a culture so vastly different from my own?

But then I thought of the protests that had begun to swell in Tehran's streets, the whispers of revolution that had grown louder with each passing day. I thought of the fear in my parents' eyes as they tried to shield me from the dangers of speaking too freely, of dreaming too boldly.

The choice wasn't just about pursuing a dream—it was about survival. Shahla had opened the door to a future I hadn't dared imagine, and walking through it began to feel less like an option and more like a necessity.

The Emotional Pull of Home

In the weeks that followed, the idea of leaving consumed me. I began to notice the little things about my life in Iran—the things I would miss if I left. The comforting hum of the azan calling worshippers to prayer. The scent of saffron and rosewater wafting from my mother's kitchen. The laughter of my sibling as we argued over who would get the last piece of lavash bread.

Every memory, every interaction, felt heavier with the knowledge that I might soon be leaving it all behind. Conversations with my parents became more poignant, their words laced with unspoken fears. My mother, ever the emotional anchor of our family, struggled to hide her sadness.

"You're my son," she said one evening, her voice breaking as she placed her hand on mine. "How can I watch you go so far away? What if I never see you again?"

Her pain was palpable, and it cut me deeply. But even as guilt gnawed at me, the seed Shahla had planted continued to grow, fueled by the belief that staying in Iran would mean sacrificing the future I so desperately wanted.

The Quiet Resolve

By the end of the summer, my decision had been made. I would leave. The path ahead was uncertain, and the thought of stepping into the unknown terrified me. But the alternative—staying in a country descending into chaos, where my dreams would be stifled by forces beyond my control—was even more frightening.

Shahla's visit had been more than just a family reunion. It had been a turning point, a moment when the horizon expanded and revealed a path I hadn't seen before. Her stories, encouragement, and unwavering belief in my potential gave me the courage to take the first step toward a life that, until then, had only existed in my imagination.

As the summer drew to a close, I stood on the brink of a monumental change. The idea of leaving home, of saying goodbye to everything familiar, filled me with a mix of dread and hope. But deep down, I knew that this was my chance to chase the possibilities Shahla had so vividly described—a chance to build a life that was my own.

A Growing Desire to Leave

For as long as I could remember, I had been captivated by the idea of life beyond Iran's borders. The West, with its promises of opportunity and freedom, had always felt like a distant beacon. But until 1978, this dream of leaving had been more of an abstraction—a vision of adventure and self-discovery. The unrest changed everything. Suddenly, the idea of leaving was no longer just a dream but a necessity. Each protest, each clash between demonstrators and police, each whispered rumor of what might come next added a new layer of urgency to my plans.

The streets I had once walked with confidence now felt foreign—hostile. Shops closed early; their owners afraid of violence erupting without warning. Posters of the Shah were defaced overnight, replaced by slogans calling for revolution. The faces of strangers were tense, their eyes darting nervously as if searching for threats in every shadow. Conversations at home and with friends shifted from dreams of the future to fears of survival.

The walls of Tehran, both literal and metaphorical, began to close in on me. I found myself looking at maps with a sense of longing, tracing imaginary paths to places I had never been but somehow felt destined to see. America, with its sprawling cities and boundless opportunities, loomed large in my imagination. I devoured every article, film, and story about life in the West, filling my mind with images of freedom and possibility. But the reality of leaving was far more complicated than I had imagined.

The Weight of Saying Goodbye

The decision to leave Iran was not one I took lightly. It meant leaving behind everything I had ever known: the comforting smell of my mother's cooking, the familiar cadence of Farsi spoken in the streets, the music that had been the soundtrack of my youth. It meant saying goodbye to family and friends, to the small rituals that had defined my life. Every farewell was a wound, a reminder of the price I would pay for pursuing a future far from home.

The conversations with my parents were some of the most difficult of my life. My father, a proud and stoic man, tried to mask his fear with practicality, urging me to focus on logistics and paperwork. My mother, always the emotional heart of our family, could not hide her heartbreak. Her eyes welled with tears every time she looked at me, as if memorizing my face in case I never returned.

"I want you to be safe," she said one evening, her voice trembling. "But what is safety if it means losing your family, your home, your identity?"

I had no answer for her, only the painful conviction that staying in Iran was no longer an option. The country I loved was changing into something unrecognizable, and I could not see a future for myself within its borders.

Dreams and Doubts

The idea of leaving Iran was like standing on the edge of a vast, uncharted sea. On one side was everything I had ever known— my family, my friends, the comforting rhythms of life in my homeland. On the other was a distant shore filled with possibility, excitement, and the promise of a better future. The decision to leave wasn't just about geography; it was about identity, about uprooting the essence of who I was to plant it in foreign soil.

The Weight of the Unknown

The prospect of moving to America filled me with equal parts exhilaration and dread. I would wake up some mornings brimming with excitement, imagining myself strolling through grand university campuses, my mind alive with new ideas, surrounded by people from all corners of the world. Other days, the doubts would come crashing down like waves on a rocky shore.

Could I really adapt to life in a country where I would be an outsider, where I didn't fully understand the language, and where my name alone might mark me as foreign? Would I ever feel at home again? The thought of starting over—of being just another immigrant in a land where no one knew my story— was both humbling and terrifying.

The questions gnawed at me in quiet moments. How would I manage without the familiar faces of my family to lean on? What if I failed? What if I didn't belong?

The Allure of Freedom

Yet, no matter how strong the doubts, the allure of America shone brighter. The country loomed large in my imagination, not as a physical place but as a concept—a land where dreams could be turned into reality. It wasn't just about escaping the chaos of Iran; it was about stepping into a world where the rules seemed different, where hard work and ambition could rewrite the script of your life.

I pictured myself walking through tree-lined campuses, a bookbag slung over my shoulder, soaking up knowledge and meeting people who shared my hunger for growth. I imagined late-night conversations with classmates from places I'd only read about, learning from their stories as much as I did from lectures.

America was freedom in every sense of the word—not just political freedom, but the freedom to be myself, to forge my own path without the weight of societal expectations or political unrest. The thought of building a life defined by possibility was intoxicating, almost dizzying in its intensity.

Conversations of Longing

My friends and I often found ourselves caught in a loop of wistful conversations about leaving Iran. On warm summer nights, as we sat on the rooftops of our homes or huddled in cozy cafés, we shared our dreams like secrets too precious to say aloud in the presence of others.

"We could be anything," one friend would say, his voice tinged with hope. "An engineer in Germany, a doctor in Canada, a musician in America. Imagine what we could do if we didn't have to deal with... this."

"This" was the unspoken weight of our reality—the protests, the arrests, the suffocating fear that hung over everything.

"I want to see the world," I'd often say, my words half a declaration, half a question. "Not just the buildings and the monuments, but the way people live, the way they think. I want to be part of something bigger."

But behind our bold words were unspoken fears. Leaving meant more than just boarding a plane. It meant walking away from the life we'd built, from the people we loved, and from the places that had shaped us. It meant accepting that we might never come back.

A Closing Window

Deep down, we all knew that time was not on our side. Iran's political situation was deteriorating faster than anyone had imagined. The protests had grown larger, the government's crackdowns harsher. Every day, it felt like the walls were closing in.

The decision to leave wasn't just about ambition or adventure anymore—it was about survival. The country we had grown up in was changing before our eyes, and there was no guarantee it would be a place we could recognize, let alone thrive in, a year or even a month from now.

The urgency was palpable. Friends who had once spoken casually about leaving were now actively making plans, applying for visas, reaching out to relatives abroad. Conversations that had once felt like daydreams now carried the weight of inevitability.

"You're lucky you have Shahla," one friend said to me one evening, his tone a mix of envy and encouragement. "If I had an aunt in America, I wouldn't think twice about going. You can't waste this chance."

He was right, of course. The window of opportunity was closing, and every delay felt like a risk. The longer I stayed, the harder it would be to leave.

A Battle Within

Still, the decision tore at me. Each time I pictured myself in America, I also saw the faces of my parents, my siblings, and my friends—the people who had been my anchors, my confidants, my world. Could I really leave them behind? Could I live with the guilt of knowing I had abandoned them to a future that felt so uncertain?

The dreams of America clashed with the pull of home in an endless battle within me. The excitement of the unknown was tempered by the fear of loss, the thrill of freedom by the weight of responsibility.

Yet, even in my moments of deepest doubt, I couldn't shake the feeling that staying in Iran would mean letting go of something even greater—my potential, my future, my chance to create a life defined by more than circumstance.

The choice wasn't simple, and it wasn't easy. But as the days passed and the cracks in Iran's stability grew wider, the path before me became clearer. I had to leave. Not because I wanted to, but because I had to.

The dreams I carried were too big for the confines of a country on the brink of revolution. And so, with a heart full of hope and fear, I began to prepare for the journey that would change my life forever.

Family Struggles

The dream of leaving Iran and starting anew in America wasn't mine alone—it was a vision that carried the hopes and fears of my entire family. For me, it symbolized opportunity and freedom. For them, it meant sacrifice, loss, and uncertainty. The clash of perspectives created a storm within our home, one that would test our bonds and redefine our relationships forever.

A Mother's Determination

My mother was the first to recognize the significance of what was unfolding. She saw the writing on the wall—the protests, the crackdowns, the whispers of revolution that grew louder with each passing day. To her, the future of Iran was clouded with too much risk and unpredictability.

"You're young," she said one evening as we sat together in the kitchen, her hands busy peeling potatoes for dinner. "You have your whole life ahead of you. You need to go, to make something of yourself while you still can."

Her voice was calm, but her eyes betrayed the weight of her emotions. This wasn't just about giving me her blessing; it was about letting go. As much as she believed in my potential, the thought of me leaving tore at her heart.

Quietly but resolutely, she began to prepare for my departure. She sold her jewelry—pieces she had cherished for years, gifts from her own mother and my father. She clipped coupons, cut corners on household expenses, and saved every spare rial. I watched her sacrifice with a mix of gratitude and guilt, knowing how much she was giving up to make my dream possible.

A Father's Resistance

My father, on the other hand, couldn't bring himself to support the idea. A man of deep pride and tradition, he viewed my desire to leave as a rejection—not just of Iran but of everything he had worked so hard to provide.

"Why do you want to run away?" he asked one night, his voice tinged with frustration and hurt. "This is your home. This is where you belong."

To him, leaving felt like abandonment. He had spent his entire life building a foundation for our family, weathering hardships, and navigating a system that often felt stacked against him. The thought of me turning my back on that legacy—on *him*—was something he couldn't reconcile.

But his resistance ran deeper than pride. He was afraid. My father was a practical man, and the idea of sending his son halfway across the world, to a place he barely understood, filled him with dread.

"What do you know about America?" he said during one of our heated arguments. "You'll be alone there. No family, no support. What if something happens to you? Who will help you then?"

I tried to reassure him, to explain that this wasn't about rejecting my roots but about expanding my horizons. But the words felt hollow in the face of his fears.

A House Divided

The tension between my parents created a rift in our household. They had always been a team, and their partnership was a source of strength for our family. But this decision put them at odds, and the arguments became a regular occurrence.

"I'm not saying it will be easy," my mother would insist, her voice firm but measured. "But we have to think about his future. Do you want him to stay here and watch his dreams die?"

"And what about *us*?" my father would counter. "What about this family? He is our son. He belongs here, not in some foreign country where he'll forget who he is."

Their arguments echoed through the house, leaving me caught in the middle. I felt like a rope in a tug-of-war, pulled between my mother's unwavering support and my father's deep-seated fears.

The Quiet Sacrifices

While the arguments raged on, my mother worked quietly in the background. She sold more than just jewelry—she parted with sentimental keepsakes, things that held memories of her own youth, her own family. She didn't tell my father about all of it; she knew he wouldn't approve.

There were moments when I wanted to tell her to stop, to let me figure it out on my own. But I couldn't. I saw the determination in her eyes, the belief she had in my potential, and I knew I couldn't let her down.

One afternoon, I caught her wrapping up a small package. Inside was a silver bracelet that had belonged to her grandmother.

"You're selling this too?" I asked, my voice heavy with guilt.

She paused, her hands trembling slightly as she tied the string around the package.

"This bracelet is just an object," she said softly. "But you? You are my son. If this helps you build a better future, it's worth it."

A Turning Point

The turning point came late one evening after another heated argument. My father, exhausted and visibly emotional, sat down at the kitchen table and stared at me for a long moment.

"If you leave," he said quietly, "promise me one thing."

"Anything," I replied, my heart pounding in my chest.

"Promise me you won't forget who you are," he said. "Promise me you'll remember where you come from, that you'll honor this family and this country, no matter where you go."

His words were a mixture of resignation and love, a reluctant acceptance of the path I had chosen.

"I promise," I said, my voice cracking under the weight of the moment.

Bittersweet Farewell

As the day of my departure drew closer, the atmosphere in our home shifted. The arguments ceased, replaced by a heavy silence that spoke volumes. My mother busied herself with preparations, packing my bags with care and slipping in small tokens—a family photo, a handwritten note, a box of sweets to remind me of home.

My father, ever the stoic, avoided goodbyes. But on the morning of my departure, as I stood by the door with my suitcase in hand, he pulled me into a tight embrace.

"Go," he said, his voice thick with emotion. "Make us proud."

The journey ahead was uncertain, but as I left my home that day, I carried with me the weight of their sacrifices, their fears, and their unwavering love. It was a burden and a blessing, a reminder of everything I was leaving behind and everything I hoped to achieve.

Navigating the Bureaucracy

Once my mandatory military draft duty was completed, I found myself facing the daunting logistics of leaving Iran. The dream of a new life in America, which had once felt so distant and intangible, was now dependent on paperwork, connections, and an endless stream of bureaucratic hurdles. Every step of the process felt like a test of my determination and resilience.

The Passport Puzzle

The first obstacle was securing a passport, a task that seemed deceptively simple on the surface but was fraught with delays and red tape. In 1978, with the country in turmoil, obtaining official documents was anything but straightforward. Offices were understaffed and overwhelmed, their employees operating under the shadow of growing unrest.

Fortunately, my uncle, who worked for Pan American Airlines, proved to be a lifeline. His connections in government circles allowed him to navigate the labyrinthine process with remarkable efficiency. He called in favors, pulling strings to ensure my application didn't languish in some forgotten pile on a bureaucrat's desk.

"Don't worry," he said, his voice steady and reassuring. "I'll make sure this goes through. Just be ready to act when the time comes."

I clung to his words, grateful for his help but acutely aware of how much was riding on his efforts. Without that passport, my plans for a new life would come to an abrupt halt before they even began.

The Visa Gauntlet

With my passport in progress, the next challenge loomed: securing a U.S. visa. In 1978, the American Embassy in Tehran was a microcosm of the chaos engulfing the country. Thousands of Iranians were desperate to leave, their dreams and fears converging in the long, serpentine lines that formed outside the embassy gates every morning.

For weeks, my friend Hoshiar and I became part of this throng. Armed with stacks of paperwork—birth certificates, financial affidavits, and a carefully prepared invitation letter from Shahla and her husband Ray—we arrived at the embassy before dawn, hoping to be among the first in line.

The wait was grueling. By the time the embassy opened its doors, the line would stretch for blocks, a living testament to the desperation of a nation on the brink. People brought blankets, thermoses of tea, and makeshift stools, settling in for what often felt like a never-ending vigil.

Camping Out in Tehran's Cool Air

Hoshiar and I quickly learned the unwritten rules of survival in that line. We took turns holding our spot while the other fetched food or stretched their legs. We carried small cushions to ease the discomfort of sitting on cold concrete for hours on end. By nightfall, the crowd would transform into an impromptu community, strangers bonding over shared stories and the mutual hope of a brighter future.

One evening, as we huddled together against the chill, Hoshiar turned to me with a nervous grin.

"Do you ever wonder," he asked, "what we'll actually find over there? What if it's nothing like we imagine?"

I laughed, though his question struck a chord.

"Even if it's not," I said, "it has to be better than this uncertainty. At least there, we'll have a chance to make something of ourselves."

Our conversations often turned philosophical in those long hours of waiting, a mix of hope and fear that mirrored the atmosphere around us. Some people shared their excitement about reuniting with family abroad or starting university. Others, like us, spoke in more abstract terms about freedom, opportunity, and the chance to escape the looming shadow of revolution.

Inside the Embassy Walls

The moment we finally stepped inside the embassy felt surreal. The air was heavy with tension, the walls lined with somber faces clutching their documents like lifelines. Embassy officials moved briskly from one window to the next, their expressions a blend of exhaustion and detachment.

When my turn came, I approached the counter with a mix of confidence and trepidation. Officer David Cook, on the other side, barely glanced at me before taking my papers.

"Purpose of your visit?" he asked, his tone clipped and businesslike.

"To study," I replied, sliding my acceptance letter and financial statements across the counter.

He nodded, flipping through the pages without much interest. The seconds stretched into minutes as he typed something into his computer. Finally, he looked up, his expression unreadable.

"Your application is complete. You'll be notified if your visa is approved."

That was it. No congratulations, no reassurance—just a vague promise that left me wondering if all the effort had been in vain.

A Moment of Triumph

When my visa was finally approved, the sense of relief and joy was overwhelming. Standing before the embassy officer, David Cook, I felt a mixture of nerves and hope. His calm demeanor and professional approach reassured me, and when he handed me my passport, stamped with the visa that would allow me to enter the United States, I felt as though a weight had been lifted off my shoulders.

Stepping out of the embassy that day, I was filled with an indescribable sense of elation. I clutched the passport tightly, unable to believe that this small document held the key to a new chapter in my life. My friends and I celebrated in the streets, laughing, hugging, and shouting in triumph.

It was a journey born of necessity and hope, a leap into the unknown fueled by the belief that the future held something better. But as I stood at the threshold of that new chapter, I couldn't shake the feeling that a part of me would always remain in the streets of Tehran, in the long embassy lines, and in the home I was about to leave behind.

The Ticket to Freedom

When the airline ticket finally arrived, it felt like a piece of magic had landed in my hands. The crisp paper with its bold letters—*Tehran to San Francisco*—seemed both impossibly real and utterly unreal at the same time. My fingers traced over the destination, lingering on the name of the city I had heard so much about but never imagined I would see with my own eyes. *San Francisco.* To me, it wasn't just a city; it was a symbol of hope, freedom, and a new beginning.

My mother regarded the ticket as if it were a sacred artifact. She handled it with such delicate care that I half-expected her to place it on an altar. Instead, she tucked it into a drawer lined with lavender sachets, her quiet ritual of preservation both touching and endearing.

"We can't let anything happen to this," she said, her voice carrying a mixture of pride and nervousness. "This is your future, your chance. We've worked so hard for this."

Her words weighed heavily on me. It wasn't just my dream anymore—it was the culmination of countless sacrifices. My mother had sold her cherished jewelry to help pay for my journey, her small gold bangles and the turquoise ring she had worn since her youth. The sight of her bare wrists haunted me, a constant reminder of what my departure truly cost.

The Countdown Begins

With the ticket in hand, the countdown to my departure began. Each passing day felt like an hourglass tipping over, the sands of time slipping away faster than I could comprehend. My life in Tehran, once so stable and predictable, now felt like it was unraveling in slow motion.

I found myself swinging between two extremes. Some moments, I would sit by the window, staring out at the bustling streets of Tehran, imagining myself walking through an entirely different world: the towering skyscrapers, the Golden Gate Bridge, and the vibrant streets of San Francisco. I envisioned the people I would meet, the university lectures I would attend, and the endless opportunities that awaited me.

But then, there were the quieter, darker moments. Late at night, when the house was silent and the weight of what I was about to do pressed down on me, I was gripped by an almost paralyzing fear. Leaving Tehran wasn't just about changing geography—it was about leaving behind my family, my culture, and the only life I had ever known.

A Farewell in Every Gesture

The days leading up to my departure were filled with goodbyes, though not always in words. My mother began cooking my favorite meals with an almost obsessive frequency, as if trying to infuse every bite with the love she couldn't physically give me once I was gone. She lingered in the doorway of my room more often, her presence a silent reassurance.

My father, ever stoic, avoided talking about my departure altogether. Instead, he showed his emotions through quiet gestures—a pat on the shoulder, a cup of tea left on my desk, and a rare nod of approval when he caught me poring over my English grammar book. I knew he didn't agree with my decision to leave, but his resistance had softened into a resigned acceptance.

My younger sibling didn't fully grasp the gravity of what was happening. To them, it seemed like an adventure I was embarking on, a storybook journey. They peppered me with questions:

"Will you see movie stars in America?"

"Are the streets really made of gold?"

I smiled and humored them, even as my heart ached at the thought of leaving their wide-eyed innocence behind.

Packing the Pieces of a Life

Packing was another emotional minefield. My suitcase became a battleground between practicality and sentimentality. My mother insisted on filling it with jars of saffron, dried herbs, and enough homemade flatbread to last a month. "You won't find food like this there," she warned, her voice trembling.

I tucked in a few cherished items of my own: a worn copy of Rumi's poetry, a cassette tape of my favorite songs, and a small photo album filled with snapshots of my life in Tehran. Each item felt like a thread connecting me to the home I was about to leave, a lifeline to my identity.

The Night Before

The night before my flight, I couldn't sleep. I sat on the rooftop of our house, staring out at the city that had shaped me. The streets were quiet, a rare stillness settling over Tehran. From my vantage point, I could see the distant glow of city lights and hear the occasional bark of a dog or the hum of a passing car.

My mind raced with questions. Would I fit in? Would I succeed? What if I failed? What if I couldn't come back?

My mother joined me after a while, wrapping a shawl around her shoulders as she settled beside me. For a long time, we didn't speak. Finally, she broke the silence.

"You'll be okay," she said, her voice firm. "You're strong. You're ready."

I nodded, though I wasn't sure I believed her.

The Morning of Departure

When the morning came, it felt like stepping into a dream—or a nightmare. The house was awake but eerily quiet, the kind of silence that accompanies profound change. My mother hugged me so tightly at the airport that I thought she might never let go.

"Don't forget us," she whispered, tears streaming down her face.

I promised her I wouldn't, though the lump in my throat made it hard to speak. My father shook my hand firmly, his eyes betraying the emotions his stoic face refused to show.

As I boarded the plane, my heart felt like it was being pulled in two directions. Each step down the aisle brought me closer to a new beginning but further from the life I had always known. When the plane took off, the city of Tehran stretched out beneath me, its streets and rooftops fading into the distance.

For the first time, the enormity of what I was doing hit me fully. I was leaving home—not just physically, but emotionally, culturally, and spiritually. I was stepping into the unknown, carrying with me the hopes and sacrifices of my family, the memories of a life left behind, and the fragile dream of a brighter future.

Chapter 3:
The Farewell at Mehrabad Airport

The drive to Mehrabad Airport that day felt like stepping into the pages of someone else's story. I sat in the back seat of my uncle's old Paykan, the upholstery worn and slightly frayed, as the car weaved through the streets of Tehran. Normally, I would have been caught up in the pulse of the city—the lively banter of shopkeepers, the playful shouts of children darting across alleyways, the steady hum of the city's endless motion. But today was different.

Every sound, every sight, every smell seemed to carry the weight of goodbye. The familiar streets, once vibrant with life and possibility, now felt like a series of snapshots in a rapidly fading memory. The city was alive with its usual chaos: impatient drivers honking their horns, vendors calling out their wares, and pedestrians navigating the crowded sidewalks with practiced ease. Yet, I felt like an outsider in my own home, detached and watching it all unfold as if through a window.

A City Etched in Memory

I stared out the car window, memorizing every detail as if I could etch the city into my soul. There was the bustling bazaar where I had haggled for trinkets with friends, the shadow of Alborz Mountains looming in the distance, and the dusty square where I had once flown kites as a boy. Even the scent of Tehran felt heightened that day—a unique mix of dust, diesel, and the faint sweetness of jasmine from the gardens that lined the quieter streets.

Each turn brought us closer to the airport and further from the life I had known. The street vendors selling hot samosas and grilled corn waved to passersby, their voices filled with an energy I envied. Life in Tehran was continuing without pause, oblivious to the fact that, for me, this was the end of an era.

The Weight of the Drive

Inside the car, silence hung heavy, punctuated only by the occasional cough from my uncle or the sound of tires crunching over uneven pavement. My mother sat beside me, clutching her purse with both hands, her knuckles pale. She kept glancing at me out of the corner of her eye; her lips pressed tightly together as if holding back the torrent of emotions threatening to spill over.

My father sat in the front passenger seat, staring straight ahead. His face was a mask of stoicism, but I could see the tension in his jaw and the way his hands gripped his knees just a little too tightly. My younger sister, who had begged to come along despite our protests, sat between us, fidgeting with the hem of her dress.

I wanted to speak, to break the silence with some words of reassurance or gratitude, but every time I opened my mouth, the words dissolved before I could form them. What could I possibly say that would make this easier for any of us?

Mehrabad Airport: A Threshold

When we finally arrived at Mehrabad Airport, it felt like stepping onto the edge of two worlds. The terminal loomed ahead, stark and imposing against the gray sky, its utilitarian design a sharp contrast to the emotional turmoil bubbling beneath the surface.

The parking lot was a sea of cars, the air thick with the mingling scents of gasoline and rain-dampened asphalt. Families crowded the entrance, their voices a chaotic symphony of laughter, tears, and hurried goodbyes. It seemed as though the entire city was converging here, each person carrying their own story of departure or arrival.

Inside the terminal, the atmosphere was even more overwhelming. The announcements crackled over the intercom in Persian and English, blending with the sound of shuffling feet and rolling suitcases. My family moved as one, a tight unit navigating the throng of travelers. My mother's hand never left my arm, as if letting go would mean losing me forever.

The Final Moments

As we reached the check-in counter, the reality of my departure began to sink in. The clerk behind the desk took my ticket and passport, her face impassive as she processed the paperwork that would officially mark my transition from one life to another. My hands felt clammy as I accepted my boarding pass, the small rectangle of paper suddenly unbearably heavy.

We stood together near the security checkpoint, where travelers said their final goodbyes. My mother's composure finally cracked as she pulled me into an embrace so tight it felt like she was trying to fuse us together. Her tears soaked through my shirt, her muffled sobs breaking what little resolve I had left.

"Be safe," she whispered, her voice trembling. "Promise me you'll take care of yourself."

I nodded, unable to speak past the lump in my throat.

My father's farewell was quieter, but no less poignant. He extended his hand, his grip firm but lingering. "Make us proud," he said, his voice steady but his eyes betraying a depth of emotion he rarely showed.

Even my sister, usually so carefree, clung to my waist, her small frame shaking with quiet sobs. "Write to us," she pleaded. "Tell us everything."

Crossing the Threshold

When the time came to walk through the security checkpoint, it felt like stepping off a cliff. I turned back one last time, my family a tableau of heartbreak and hope. My mother waved, tears streaming down her face. My father stood rigid, his hand resting protectively on my sister's shoulder.

As I moved further away, the distance between us seemed to stretch like an unbridgeable chasm. The sounds of the terminal faded into the background, replaced by the deafening roar of my own heartbeat.

By the time I reached the gate, I was overwhelmed by a strange mix of emotions: grief, excitement, fear, and determination. Boarding the plane, I took one last look at the city through the terminal window. Tehran stretched out beneath the fading light, its streets and rooftops shimmering like a mosaic of memories.

When the plane lifted off, I felt both untethered and unbearably heavy, as if I had left a piece of myself behind. The city, my family, my past—they were all shrinking below me, becoming part of a story I would carry with me, but never fully relive.

In that moment, I understood the true weight of leaving home. It wasn't just a journey to a new country—it was the start of an entirely new life, one that would forever be shaped by the place I had left behind.

On the Plane: A Journey Begins

The plane's engines roared to life, vibrating through the cabin as if echoing the storm of emotions swirling inside me. The seatbelt tightened around my waist, a physical reminder that there was no turning back now. I glanced at Hoshiar, who sat beside me with a wide grin plastered across his face. His energy was infectious, a mix of excitement and nervous anticipation that mirrored my own.

"Ready for the adventure?" he asked, his tone light but his eyes betraying the same uncertainty I felt.

"Not really," I admitted, though I couldn't help but match his grin. The words felt both true and false, as if I were caught between two realities—the one I was leaving and the one I was hurtling toward.

The Final Glimpse

As the plane began to taxi down the runway, I turned to the window, my heart pounding. Outside, Mehrabad Airport's terminal lights glowed softly against the night sky, a beacon in the darkness. Beyond them lay Tehran, its streets and rooftops illuminated by the warm, flickering glow of streetlights and late-night fires burning in metal drums.

This was the city that had cradled my childhood dreams, the place where I had laughed, loved, and learned to navigate the complexities of life. Now, it was slipping away, a glittering tapestry that seemed to stretch endlessly until it faded into the horizon.

The engines roared louder, the plane picking up speed. My pulse quickened in tandem, and before I knew it, we were airborne. The moment the wheels left the ground, my chest tightened. Tehran grew smaller, its lights scattering like fireflies in the distance. I pressed my forehead to the cold glass of the window, unwilling to look away until the city disappeared entirely.

The Weight of Departure

The climb into the sky felt endless, each second pulling me further away from everything I had ever known. I gripped the armrests, not out of fear of flying but from the sheer weight of the moment. It was real now—this journey, this leap into the unknown. I was no longer tethered to the familiar streets of Tehran, to the voices of my family, or to the life I had once taken for granted.

My thoughts raced. What was my mother doing at this moment? Was she still standing at the terminal window, watching the plane disappear into the night? Was my father holding back his tears, stoic as ever, while my sister clung to his side?

A pang of guilt washed over me, sharp and unrelenting. I had chosen this path for myself, but it felt like I had taken a piece of them with me, leaving behind a void I could never truly fill.

Finding Small Comforts

As the plane leveled out, the cabin lights dimmed, bathing us in a soft glow. The hum of the engines settled into a steady rhythm, a strange and unexpected comfort. I exhaled deeply, releasing some of the tension that had coiled tightly in my chest.

Hoshiar nudged me again, this time offering a small packet of dates he had tucked into his bag. "For good luck," he said with a wink.

I took one, the sweetness of the fruit contrasting with the bittersweetness of the moment. Around us, passengers murmured in low tones, their voices blending with the faint hiss of the air vents. Somewhere near the back of the plane, someone began to hum a soft tune—a Persian lullaby that felt achingly familiar. The melody drifted through the cabin, wrapping itself around me like a warm embrace.

A Glimmer of Hope

For the first time that night, I allowed myself to think of the possibilities that lay ahead. The plane wasn't just carrying me away from my past—it was carrying me toward a future I had only dared to imagine. I thought of San Francisco, the city whose name felt like a promise. I thought of the university campuses I had seen in magazines, of the people I would meet, the stories I would tell, and the life I would build.

The fear and sadness didn't vanish, but they softened, making room for something else—hope. The kind of hope that stirs in the quiet moments when the world feels vast and full of promise.

I leaned back in my seat, the hum of the engines a steady companion as I closed my eyes. I was leaving behind a chapter of my life, but ahead of me stretched blank pages, waiting to be filled. The thought was both terrifying and exhilarating, and for the first time that night, I let myself smile.

The journey had just begun.

Chapter 4:
The First Glimpse of San Francisco

The faint hum of the airplane engines lingered in my ears as I climbed into the backseat of Shahla and Ray's car, the leather upholstery cools against my palms. I sank into the seat, my body weighed down by exhaustion but my mind too restless to fully surrender to it. The journey from Tehran to America had drained me in ways I couldn't yet articulate—physically, emotionally, and spiritually. I felt as if I had been uprooted, torn from the soil of familiarity and thrust into a world that was dazzlingly foreign.

The car's engine purred as we merged onto the freeway, its rhythmic vibrations syncing with the muffled cadence of Shahla and Ray's conversation in the front seat. They spoke in a mix of English and Farsi, their words washing over me like waves. I caught fragments—directions, mentions of "home," and an occasional inquiry into how I was feeling. But I couldn't summon the energy to respond.

I gazed out the window, the city's lights illuminating the darkness like scattered constellations. San Francisco was still a distant name on the road signs, but already, the atmosphere felt alive. The roads stretched wide and smooth, bordered by towering streetlights that cast a golden glow over the steady stream of cars. I pressed my forehead against the glass, the coolness grounding me as my thoughts whirled.

A Mind Adrift

Exhaustion threatened to pull me under, but I clung to consciousness, afraid of missing even a moment of this new world. Memories from the past days floated to the surface like fragments of a dream: the tear-streaked faces of my family at Mehrabad Airport, the long hours waiting at the gate, the surreal moment when the plane left the ground and Tehran became a patchwork of lights below.

I had felt untethered then, as if the ascension into the clouds had severed the last ties binding me to my homeland. That same feeling lingered now, amplified by the alien surroundings. Everything outside the car window was unfamiliar, from the architecture of the buildings to the bright, bold billboards advertising products I didn't recognize. Even the air smelled different—crisper, cleaner, but missing the earthy, familiar scent of Tehran's streets.

The Bay Bridge: A Dreamlike Passage

I must have dozed off, lulled by the steady hum of the car and the exhaustion of a journey that felt both endless and transformative. When I opened my eyes, the world outside the window had shifted into something surreal. Towering steel beams, their silhouettes outlined by dim, golden light, rose and fell as Shahla's car glided smoothly along the Bay Bridge. The beams crisscrossed above us, creating a geometric pattern that seemed to stretch into eternity.

The bridge loomed vast and otherworldly, a strange amalgamation of strength and elegance. Below, the bay's dark waters mirrored faint glimmers of light, their surface rippled by unseen currents. The air inside the car felt heavier, charged with a strange energy that made my chest tighten. For a moment, I couldn't tell if I was awake or still dreaming.

I rubbed my eyes, trying to shake off the haze of sleep, but the disorientation lingered. The bridge felt alien—like a corridor leading not to a city but to another world entirely. Half-dreaming, my thoughts spiraled into absurdity: *Does everyone in San Francisco live underground?* The muted glow of the bridge's lights, the weighty steel frame, and the enveloping darkness all seemed to suggest some vast subterranean expanse.

A Quiet Laughter

The thought was so ridiculous that I let out a soft laugh, half-amused and half-embarrassed by the strangeness of my own imagination. The sound broke the silence in the car, catching Shahla's attention. She glanced back at me in the rearview mirror, her smile as warm and familiar as the scent of home.

"What's so funny?" she asked, her voice light and curious, cutting through the otherworldly stillness.

I hesitated, torn between sharing my absurd musings and keeping them to myself. But something about her tone—reassuring and free of judgment—made me speak.

"I...I thought maybe everyone here lives underground," I said, my voice tinged with self-conscious humor. The words felt strange as they left my mouth, but the honesty of them brought a small, wry smile to my face.

Shahla's laughter bubbled up immediately, genuine and melodic. It filled the car, a sound so familiar and comforting that it momentarily banished the strangeness of the bridge. "Underground?" she repeated, shaking her head with amusement. "No, no. San Francisco is very much above ground. Just wait—you'll see for yourself soon enough."

An Emerging Vision

Her words carried a promise, and I clung to them as I turned my gaze back to the bridge. The steel beams, now bathed in the amber glow of the passing streetlights, no longer felt oppressive but protective, as though they were guiding me safely to the other side.

The car continued its journey, the rhythmic click of tires crossing seams in the bridge blending with the muffled sounds of the bay below. The faint outline of the city began to emerge in the distance, its lights twinkling like stars scattered across a dark canvas.

I leaned forward slightly, straining to make out the shapes and contours of this fabled city. My heart beat faster, a mix of anticipation and apprehension. This wasn't just a physical crossing; it was a passage from one life to another. Behind me lay the familiar streets of Tehran, the echo of my mother's whispered prayers, and the bittersweet weight of goodbye. Ahead of me was the unknown—a city that held both promise and challenge, a place where I would have to build a new life from the ground up.

A Threshold of Change

As we neared the end of the bridge, the cityscape grew clearer. Skyscrapers rose against the horizon, their windows reflecting the golden glow of the bridge's lights. Cars sped past us, their headlights streaking through the darkness like fleeting fireflies.

The pang of disappointment I had felt earlier gave way to something more profound—a realization that this moment marked a threshold. The Bay Bridge wasn't just a means of transportation; it was a symbol, a reminder that I was leaving one world behind to step into another.

As the car exited the bridge and merged onto the streets of San Francisco, I sat back and let the city unfold before me. The dreamlike quality of the passage lingered, but now, it was infused with a quiet determination. For better or worse, I was here. The journey across the bridge was over, but the real journey was only beginning.

The Weight of Silence

As we crossed the bridge, the car's interior fell silent. Even Shahla and Ray seemed to sense the gravity of the moment. I stared out the window, watching the lights of the city come into sharper focus. Skyscrapers loomed in the distance, their outlines softened by the night, while the Bay shimmered beneath the bridge like a vast, restless mirror.

For the first time since I left Tehran, the enormity of what I had done began to sink in. I wasn't just visiting a new place; I was starting over. The life I had known—the language, the culture, the people—was now behind me, and ahead lay a future that felt as uncertain as it did exhilarate.

I thought of my parents and sister, wondering what they were doing at that exact moment. Were they sitting together in the courtyard, sipping tea under the stars, their hearts heavy with my absence? The thought was both comforting and heart-wrenching, a reminder of the sacrifice embedded in my journey.

A New Beginning

"Not much longer now," Shahla said, turning in her seat to smile at me. Her words were meant to reassure, but they carried an undertone of finality.

The car exited the freeway and began winding through quieter streets lined with houses that seemed to exude warmth. The architecture was unlike anything I had seen in Tehran—Victorian-style homes with steep roofs and bay windows, their facades painted in soft pastels. They stood shoulder to shoulder, illuminated by porch lights that glowed like tiny beacons in the dark.

When we finally arrived, Shahla turned to me again. "Welcome to your new home," she said softly.

I stepped out of the car and into the cool night air. The house was modest but inviting, with a small porch adorned with potted plants. As I stood there, suitcase in hand, I felt an unexpected wave of emotion. This was it—the beginning of a life I had dreamed about for years.

I didn't know what challenges lay ahead or how much I would miss the world I had left behind. But in that moment, beneath the sprawling sky of San Francisco, I felt a flicker of hope. For all its uncertainty, the future was mine to shape.

The First Sight of the City

Emerging from the Bay Bridge felt like surfacing from a long, disorienting dream, my mind still hazy from the journey and the emotional weight of leaving everything behind. As the car descended from the towering structure, the city of San Francisco unfolded before me, stretching out like a glittering treasure chest spilled across the hills.

The scene before me was unlike anything I had ever imagined. Thousands of lights twinkled against the deep indigo sky, each one an individual star that formed a sprawling constellation. The city's iconic skyline, jagged and imposing, loomed on the horizon like a living, breathing entity. The buildings—tall, angular, and imposing—seemed to rise out of the ground, their illuminated windows glowing like stars caught in a web of steel and glass. Every street, every corner, was bathed in the flickering light of neon signs, casting a colorful glow over the people who bustled along below. San Francisco was not just a city; it was a force of nature, alive and pulsing with an energy I could feel deep in my chest, as though the very ground beneath me was vibrating in sync with my rapid heartbeat.

A Reality Unlike the Dream

This was my first glimpse of America, the land I had longed for, the place I had heard so much about. Yet, it was nothing like the America I had envisioned back in Tehran. My dreams of the West had been built from the glossy photos in magazines, the movies that portrayed idyllic lives filled with wide, sunlit boulevards, pristine homes surrounded by white picket fences, and impossibly happy families. In my mind, America was clean, perfect, and orderly—a sharp contrast to the complexities and contradictions of Iran. But the San Francisco before me was raw, gritty, and unapologetically real. Its beauty was unpolished, and yet there was a magnetism to it that took my breath away. This wasn't the fairy tale I had imagined, but it was something far more compelling.

As the car wound through the city's labyrinthine streets, I couldn't help but be struck by how alive everything felt, even this late at night. The air hummed with a kind of quiet urgency as though the city itself never stopped moving. Neon signs flickered and buzzed outside diners and small storefronts, their colors popping against the darkness like bright, painted brushstrokes on a black canvas. Couples walked hand-in-hand, their laughter and conversation carrying through the cool night air. The occasional burst of music drifted from open windows, mingling with the rhythm of footsteps on the pavement. The sound of life, of the city's heartbeat, was inescapable.

A Flicker of Hope

I leaned back against the cool seat, the city unfolding around me like an unfamiliar but intriguing dream. For the first time since leaving Tehran, I felt something other than fear or sadness. I felt a flicker of excitement, a spark of possibility. The city was vast and overwhelming, but it was also full of promise. There was a sense of freedom in the air, a feeling that anything was possible here—something I hadn't dared to believe back in Iran, where the walls of oppression had always felt too close.

I nodded, though I wasn't sure she could see. My eyes were fixed on the city ahead, drinking it in, absorbing every detail. This was the beginning of something new, something frightening but also exhilarating. The unfamiliarity of it all— the streets, the sounds, the people—felt overwhelming at first, but there was also a strange sense of freedom in being a stranger in a strange land.

I had crossed an ocean to get here, leaving behind a world that, for all its beauty, was slipping away from me. Now, as I looked at the city that would become my new home, I realized something important: no matter how much I had left behind, the future was still mine to create. And in San Francisco, with its raw beauty and its ceaseless energy, I could already feel the first steps of my new life beginning to take shape.

The Drive to Concord

As we left the heart of San Francisco behind, the glittering skyline slowly dissolved into the night, and the pulse of the city was replaced by something altogether quieter. The vibrant energy of the streets faded, leaving behind a stillness that seemed almost too peaceful after the whirlwind of the city. The contrast was jarring—one moment I was surrounded by the roar of life, the hum of traffic, the unceasing flow of people; the next, I found myself speeding down suburban streets that stretched on endlessly, the occasional streetlamp casting pale pools of light onto the asphalt. The towering buildings of the city were replaced by neat rows of houses, each one trimmed in identical fashion, each one nestled quietly behind manicured lawns. The tree-lined avenues appeared almost like a dream— a vision of an America I had only imagined in stories, one that seemed tranquil and secure. The headlights from Shahla's car illuminated the road ahead, throwing long shadows that seemed to shift and flicker with every curve in the road, almost like the city itself was bidding me farewell.

As the car wound its way through the suburban sprawl, the shift in atmosphere was palpable. The constant hum of the city was replaced by a heavy silence, broken only by the faint rustle of leaves in the wind and the soft murmur of Shahla and Ray's voices in the front seat. Their conversation flowed gently between them, but I barely heard their words. My mind was far away, lost in a tangle of thoughts and emotions. The further we drove, the more the tension in my chest began to unwind. The exhaustion that had clung to me throughout the journey began to settle in, but it was a different kind of weariness now—a weariness that carried a strange sense of relief. It wasn't just the relief of having finally made it across the globe to America; it was the relief of having left behind the turbulence of Iran, the weight of uncertainty, and the fear of what the future might hold. The quiet was a balm to my overactive thoughts, and for the first time since leaving Tehran, I allowed myself to relax.

I leaned my head back against the seat, watching the dark trees blur past the windows. The road ahead stretched endlessly, disappearing into the distance. There was no turning back now. The world I had known was thousands of miles away, and I was here, in this foreign land, in a place where everything was new and unknown. I closed my eyes, trying to calm my racing heart. Shahla and Ray's voices became a distant lullaby, a steady, comforting backdrop as I fought to keep my thoughts from spiraling.

Arriving at Shahla and Ray's Home

When we finally pulled into the driveway, a profound sense of arrival washed over me. The car stopped in front of a modest house that seemed to glow warmly in the dark. Its yellow light spilled from the windows, spilling onto the neatly kept lawn, casting long shadows against the neatly trimmed hedges. It was a far cry from the grandeur of the places I had imagined living in, but in that moment, it was everything I needed.

The house was simple and unpretentious, but there was a warmth that felt like a welcome, as though the building understood the journey I had made. Shahla turned to me, her smile warm and reassuring, and for a moment, I saw the kindness in her eyes, the quiet strength that had always been there for me.

"Welcome home," she said, her voice soft, laced with a tenderness that made my throat tighten.

For a moment, I couldn't speak. The words hung in the air, and I felt a lump rise in my throat. Home. The word felt foreign, almost out of place. How could a place so far from everything I had ever known be called home? How could this small, quiet house replace the world I had left behind? But as I looked around, something inside me softened. There was a kind of promise in this moment—promise of safety, of peace, and of a chance to rebuild. The future, uncertain as it was, was now in my hands.

I stepped out of the car, the cool night air greeting me with a strange sense of calm. Shahla and Ray led the way, and as I followed them up to the door, I couldn't help but feel the weight of the past few weeks press in on me. The goodbye at Mehrabad Airport, the flight across continents, the overwhelming shock of arriving in a foreign country—everything had led to this moment. A new life was beginning, and though I couldn't yet see what it would look like, the first steps were already taking shape.

As I crossed the threshold into their home, a feeling of quiet certainty settled over me. This was where I would begin again. This was where my new life would start.

The Comfort of a New Home

Inside Shahla and Ray's home, the contrast to the starkness of my journey could not have been more pronounced. The warmth of the house enveloped me, and I could almost feel the tension in my shoulders begin to ease. The air was thick with the soothing aroma of spices, familiar yet foreign, mingling with the comforting scent of freshly brewed tea that seemed to embrace me like a soft blanket. Shahla had thought of everything. The moment I stepped inside, it was clear that this was a place where I could begin to heal, to breathe, and to settle into a life far removed from the chaos I had left behind in Tehran.

Shahla led me down the narrow hallway, her footsteps light on the polished floor. She stopped at a small door and pushed it open to reveal a simple but welcoming bedroom. The room was modest: a single bed draped in soft linens, a wooden desk against the wall, and a window that framed the quiet street outside. The suburban tranquility seeped in through the glass, its stillness almost surreal after the noise of Tehran. The world outside seemed calm, untouched by the tension I had fled from. It was a far cry from the homes I had envisioned myself living in—there were no grand structures or opulent furniture—but in that simplicity, I found a rare comfort. This was a space that was mine, even if only for now.

As I set my bags down and sat on the edge of the bed, I could feel the weight of the journey—both physical and emotional—press down on me. The past few days had been a blur of travel, exhaustion, and farewells, each one more difficult than the last. Leaving Tehran, stepping onto the plane with nothing but the hopes of a better future ahead, and then finally arriving in a foreign land had taken a toll on me. There was a rawness to the transition, an overwhelming feeling of displacement. But now, as I sat in this quiet room, the constant hum of uncertainty that had gnawed at me for so long began to fade, replaced by something new. Hope. It felt like a fragile seed being planted in the soil of this new life.

I leaned back against the bed, closing my eyes for a moment, allowing myself to absorb the calm. The weight of the goodbyes—the final embrace with my mother, the tearful exchange of words with friends I might never see again—still lingered in my chest. But in this room, in this home, there was a kind of peace that I hadn't felt in days. For the first time since leaving Iran, I let myself imagine the possibilities ahead. This was a new beginning. It wasn't what I had expected—nothing ever is—but it was real, and it was mine.

As I sank into the stillness, the world outside my room felt distant, and I could almost forget the chaos I had left behind. For a fleeting moment, I felt as though I had found a small corner of stability in the storm that had been my life.

Just before bed, Shahla appeared in the doorway with the phone in her hand. "It's for you," she said softly, her tone both matter-of-fact and gentle. I knew who it was before she even handed it to me. My heart clenched as I took the receiver, and I could already hear the faint crackle of my mother's voice on the other end of the line.

"Are you okay?" she asked, her voice strained with a mixture of worry and relief.

Hearing my mother's voice after everything that had happened was like a lifeline thrown across an ocean. In her words, I could feel the years of care, love, and everything she had poured into me in preparation for this moment. She was the one who had nurtured my dream, who had given me the strength to take that first step, and now she was the one I needed to reassure.

"I'm fine, Mom," I said, though my voice wavered slightly, betraying the emotions I had been trying to suppress. "I'm here, safe."

The silence on the other end of the line spoke volumes. I knew she was holding back tears, that the sadness of my departure was still raw for her, just as it was for me. But through the quiet, there was something else—something unmistakable. It was pride. I could hear it in the way she spoke, in the way she carefully chose her words.

"Take care of yourself," she said, her voice softer now, the strength in it unmistakable. "And remember, no matter where you go, you carry us with you."

I pressed the phone tightly to my ear, closing my eyes as I let her words wash over me. "I will, Mom. I promise," I whispered, my voice thick with emotion.

The call ended, and I sat there, holding the receiver in my hand, a silent tear slipping down my cheek. The ache of missing her, of missing everything I had left behind, was still there, raw and untamed. Somehow, in that moment, I understood something fundamental: I wasn't truly alone. I carried them with me, in every step I took, in every decision I made. Their love, their hopes, and their sacrifices were part of me, and no distance could ever change that.

As I finally set the phone down and lay in bed, the warmth of the house surrounding me, I knew that the path ahead would be hard, but I wasn't walking it alone. With that thought, I closed my eyes and allowed the quiet comfort of my new home to lull me into sleep.

A New Day, A New Life

The soft rays of sunlight filtered through the window the next morning, casting a warm, golden hue over the room. It was as though the light itself was gently coaxing me awake, pulling me out of the quiet, surreal fog that still lingered in my mind. I lay still for a moment, absorbing the weight of the realization that had yet to fully settle in: I was in America. For so long, it had been nothing more than a dream, a distant hope, a whispered promise. Now, it was my reality.

The room around me, modest and simple, held a strange comfort. There was no grandeur, no overwhelming display of wealth or status. It was a space that felt quiet, yet somehow, it echoed with possibility. It was a blank canvas. And for the first time in my life, I could begin to paint the picture of who I wanted to be—far from the shadow of a turbulent past and unencumbered by the constraints of a life I no longer recognized.

As I lay there, letting the stillness of the morning wrap around me, I heard movement in the kitchen. Shahla's cheerful voice floated in, calling my name with an eagerness that made me smile. She was already at work, organizing the small details of my new life. It was no surprise—she had always been the kind of person who made things happen with relentless energy. The hustle of a new beginning seemed to energize her, and she was eager to share that energy with me.

After a quick breakfast, we headed out on what felt like a whirlwind tour of practicalities. Shahla's determination was palpable as we moved from one errand to the next: getting a

California ID, signing up for a library card, and opening a bank account. Each step was both thrilling and disorienting. These were the small but significant tasks that would help me integrate into this new world, the kind of mundane rituals that people back home might have taken for granted, but for me, each was a monumental event.

In the lobby of the Crocker Bank, I found myself standing before the teller, clutching a small piece of plastic—a California bank card. It seemed so simple, yet so profound. In that moment, I realized this was the first piece of a puzzle I had been trying to solve for years. This card wasn't just a functional tool—it was a symbol. It was proof that I had arrived, that I had taken the first real step toward building a future from scratch.

I could almost hear my mother's voice in the back of my mind, the words she had spoken so many times: "You have to work hard. You have to prove yourself." Now, as I held the card in my hand, those words took on new meaning. This was my chance to build something lasting, to create a life where my efforts mattered, where ambition could take me farther than it ever could in the place I had left behind.

For a brief moment, I allowed myself to savor the feeling. I looked at the card, turning it over in my hand, almost as though trying to absorb its significance. The future stretched out before me, vast and open, filled with both uncertainty and infinite possibilities. A small smile tugged at my lips as I thought of the dreams I had once whispered to myself in the quiet of my room back in Tehran. Now, those dreams were no longer distant fantasies. They were real. They were mine.

As we left the bank and stepped into the car, I felt a quiet pride bubbling up inside me. This was a milestone. A small, everyday task, yes, but one that marked the start of a journey unlike any I had ever known. And for the first time, I felt the weight of my choice—leaving everything behind and starting anew—begin to feel lighter.

Shahla noticed the silence that had settled over me and glanced over with a knowing smile. "How does it feel?" she asked, her voice gentle, yet carrying the weight of the question.

I hesitated for a moment, choosing my words carefully. "It feels… real," I said, my voice catching slightly as I looked at the bank card once more. "I feel like I'm here. Like I finally have a chance."

Her smile widened, and she nodded. "You do. You've already taken the hardest step. Everything else will fall into place."

As we drove through the streets of Concord, past the neat homes and tree-lined avenues, the world around me seemed both familiar and foreign. There was a certain stillness to the air, a calm that felt different from the frenetic energy of Tehran. Yet, within that calm, I found a certain excitement. It wasn't the manic energy of a city filled with dreams and distractions but a quieter kind of promise. A place where I could breathe, think, and build.

The future was still uncertain, and the path ahead was unclear. But today, as I sat in Shahla's car, holding a bank card that had unlocked a small piece of this new life, I couldn't help but feel that I had already begun the process of shaping it. With each new day and step, I would get closer to becoming who I was meant to be. And that was a feeling worth holding onto—something I would carry with me through the unknowns and uncertainties that lay ahead.

Chapter 5:
Learning Through Hard Work

When I first arrived in the United States, everything was new, overwhelming, and full of possibilities. The bustling streets of San Francisco felt both exhilarating and intimidating. As a young man eager to learn, experience life, and forge my path in a land so different from the one I had known, the future seemed both uncertain and full of promise.

My time in ESL classes had been enriching. The classes helped me navigate the language barrier and build friendships, but another side to life quickly demanded my attention: I needed to make money. Living in a new country without much resources meant that my financial independence was essential. My immediate goal was clear—buying a car, the symbol of freedom and independence in the American dream. It was a tangible marker of progress, something I could work toward and claim as my own.

But the road to that car seemed steep. Not only was I still learning English, but I also had no experience navigating the American job market. I didn't know where to begin, or even if I had the skills to make it in a city as vast and competitive as San Francisco. The fear gnawed at me daily. Would I be able to communicate effectively? Would anyone hire someone with a heavy accent and little to no experience? These questions clouded my mind as I set out to search for work.

But I was determined to succeed. I had no other choice. So, each day, I walked the streets of San Francisco, hoping something—anything—would present itself. The city, for all its charm and opportunity, felt cold and indifferent to a newcomer like me. I had no network, no connections, and no real understanding of the systems that governed work here. Still, I walked, my feet carrying me through unfamiliar neighborhoods, hoping my persistence would lead me somewhere.

Then, on one of these walks, something extraordinary happened. As I strolled through the busy streets, a familiar sound—so rare in a foreign land—caught my attention. The cadence of my native language, Farsi, reached my ears. My heart skipped a beat. There, in the middle of this vast, unfamiliar city, I had overheard two men speaking in the language I had grown up with. It was a lifeline, a bridge back to home, something I hadn't expected to find in the chaos of San Francisco.

Without a second thought, I approached them. My heart raced as I mustered the courage to speak.

"Excuse me," I said, walking up to them. "I just arrived in America, and I'm looking for work."

One of the men, a tall man with a friendly face, turned to me with a welcoming smile. "Can you move carpets?" he asked simply.

In that moment, I didn't care what the job was. I needed a foot in the door. The opportunity to work, to earn my first paycheck in this new country, was more than enough. Without thinking twice, I answered, "Yes, I can."

Victor Barkhordarian, the man who spoke to me, explained that they were holding a weekend carpet sale and needed help moving and arranging carpets. It was temporary, grueling work, but to me, it felt like a step toward something much larger. This job, though physical and demanding, held a promise that I clung to. It was a chance to prove to myself that I could survive, that I could adapt, that I could make a living in this foreign land.

The weekend of the sale arrived, and I showed up ready to work. The day was long, and the work was grueling. We moved heavy carpets, rolled them up, laid them out for customers, and repeated the process over and over. My arms ached. My back throbbed. The physical toll of the labor was undeniable. Yet, in each movement, in every carpet I moved, I felt something else—a deep sense of pride. It wasn't just about the exhaustion. It was about the fact that I was there. I was working. I was making progress. Each carpet felt like a small victory, a step closer to the life I had come to build.

Victor Barkhordarian proved to be not only a boss but also a mentor. He understood that I was new to this country and that I was still learning the ropes. His patience was invaluable. With each task, he offered guidance, making sure I understood everything and helping me improve. By the end of the weekend, I had earned my first paycheck—small, but significant.

When Victor Barkhordarian handed me the check, I held it in my hand for a long moment. It wasn't just about the money. It was about the accomplishment, the first tangible proof that I could make it. I didn't care that I didn't know how much I was being paid. This check symbolized something deeper: my first success in America. The pride I felt at that moment was overwhelming.

I walked straight to Crocker Bank, eager to cash my check. The teller handed me the cash, and as I looked down at the bills in my hand, I noticed something—a small corner of one of the bills was missing. It seemed insignificant, but as I walked out of the bank and looked at that small, torn bill, something profound occurred to me. This wasn't just any dollar bill. It was the first dollar I had earned in America, a symbol of my journey. It wasn't perfect. It wasn't polished. But it was mine. And in that imperfect dollar was the promise of everything I was working toward.

I decided to keep that bill, framing it later as a reminder of that moment—the moment my life in America truly began. To this day, that framed dollar hangs in my office, a silent reminder of where it all started and how far I've come.

Yet, I knew I couldn't rely on temporary jobs forever. I needed something more stable, something that could provide the steady income I needed to sustain myself and reach my goals. So, I kept searching for work, never allowing myself to grow complacent. It wasn't long before I found an opportunity at Michael Anthony's, a nightclub in Concord. The nightlife was electric, the music pulsating through the air, and the work was light compared to the physical labor I'd done before. But there was something unsettling about it. It felt like a world apart from the stability I was looking for—a world of late nights, fleeting interactions, and the kind of work that didn't promise long-term growth.

I adapted quickly, but I knew this job wouldn't help me build the future I wanted. I had bigger dreams, and the energy of the nightclub, while exciting, couldn't sustain me forever. I needed to keep moving forward.

That's when I found a job at Cooper Skillet, a small, local restaurant where the work was steady but humble. The owner, Ahad, known to most as Hamid, was one of the kindest people I had met in America. He took me under his wing, teaching me the ropes and showing me the value of hard work in a setting where every task—no matter how small—was vital. I worked as a busboy, cleaning, vacuuming, and making sure everything was in order for the next day. It wasn't glamorous, but I took pride in it. Every action and every task completed was a statement of my dedication and my willingness to do whatever it took to succeed.

Even though I didn't have a car yet, my aunt Shahla always supported me. She would drive me to and from the restaurant, often staying up late to pick me up after a long shift. Sometimes, if it was particularly late, she would even come inside and help me with the vacuuming. Her unwavering support meant the world to me. It reminded me that I wasn't alone—that I had family here who believed in me.

Despite the long hours and exhaustion, I knew that this job, like all the others, was a stepping stone. It wasn't my final destination but an important part of my journey. And then came one of the most frightening experiences of my life.

I had taken a temporary job at a gas station. It was supposed to be easy work with flexible hours. But one night, a man walked in, pulled out a gun, and demanded money. My heart stopped. I froze. My body betrayed me, paralyzed by fear. I handed over the money, my hands shaking uncontrollably. The man took the money and left, but the shock stayed with me long after he was gone. I quit that job shortly after. The fear of that experience lingered, and I realized that I couldn't continue working in an environment that made me feel unsafe.

I learned something important that night: life is fragile, and the choices we make can shape our futures in ways we don't always anticipate.

Despite that setback, I kept moving forward. My perseverance paid off when my uncle Ray, a high-ranking officer at Levi Strauss & Co., helped me secure a job at the company. This was a turning point in my life. The job offered stability, and for the first time, I felt like I had a foothold in the future I had dreamed of.

The work at Levi's was challenging, but I embraced it. It was no longer about scraping by, hopping from one temporary job to the next. Now, I have a solid foundation to build on. Every job, every step, had taught me resilience, perseverance, and the value of hard work. I had come a long way from the man who had arrived in America with nothing but a dream. And now, with a job at Levi's, I was finally on solid ground, ready to face whatever came next.

Chapter 6:
The Emotional Journey Toward Independence

Looking back on those early months in America, I can see how the surface excitement of new experiences masked the deep emotional challenges I faced. The thrill of a new beginning, of discovering a different culture, a new language, and meeting new people, was exhilarating—but it was also daunting. The changes were not just external—they were internal, profound shifts that pushed me to confront parts of myself I had never fully known. It wasn't just about adapting to a new country. It was about navigating an emotional journey that would test every fiber of my being. I wasn't just trying to find my place in a new world; I was trying to reconcile who I was with who I was becoming in this strange new land.

At first, everything felt monumental—each decision, no matter how small, carried with it the weight of uncertainty. It was as though I was walking a tightrope, trying to balance the dreams I had brought with me against the reality I was now living. I had come to America with hope and ambition. My family had sent me here with the belief that I could build a better life, not just for myself, but for them too. They had invested so much in me—their hopes, their sacrifices, and their dreams rested on my shoulders. And yet, in the stillness of the night, when the world was quiet, and my thoughts could no longer be silenced by the noise of daily life, I often found myself questioning if I could truly live up to their expectations.

The pressure was immense, a constant weight I carried wherever I went. Was I doing enough? Was I moving forward fast enough? Would I be able to build a future that reflected the sacrifices my family had made for me to be here? Each moment of doubt felt like a luxury I could not afford, a dangerous indulgence that threatened to pull me under.

Living with Shahla and Ray during those early days was a refuge, a safe harbor amidst the storm. They were my emotional anchor, offering a space to rest when the turbulence of self-doubt and loneliness became too overwhelming. They understood that I was far from home, far from everything I had ever known, and they did their best to ease that pain. But even in their company, in their warm home where I could temporarily forget the weight of the world outside, I couldn't shake the feeling that I wasn't where I was supposed to be—not just physically, but emotionally.

I had come to America for independence, but that freedom came with a sobering realization: true independence was not just about physical separation from the familiar, but an emotional transformation that would demand everything from me. It was not just about living on my own terms; it was about confronting the internal battle of letting go of my past while trying to hold on to who I was.

Every day felt like a struggle between my desire to prove myself—to show that I could make it on my own—and the undeniable truth that I wasn't ready yet. The small victories I achieved in the outside world—finding a job, making new friends, adjusting to a new routine—were crucial steps toward independence. But they didn't ease the internal battles I faced.

They didn't take away the overwhelming loneliness that gripped me when I lay awake at night, wondering if I was doing enough.

There were days when I felt like a stranger in my own skin. I would look in the mirror and wonder who I had become. The person staring back at me seemed unfamiliar, distant. I wasn't the person I had been in Iran—confident, surrounded by family and friends, with a sense of belonging. Now, I was adrift in a vast sea of uncertainty, with only the flimsiest of lifelines to hold onto.

Even simple things, like walking down the street, felt charged with significance. Every interaction was a reminder of how different my world had become. A simple exchange at a store, a conversation with a coworker, felt like a test of my ability to adapt, to survive. And yet, in these moments, there was a quiet, almost invisible strength forming within me, though I couldn't always recognize it at the time.

Despite all the challenges, there were glimmers of hope that kept me going. Every new word I learned in English, every small success at work, every friendship I made felt like a victory in itself. But the emotional toll of constantly pushing forward, constantly trying to prove that I could survive, was exhausting. I often found myself caught between two worlds— my old life, which I could never fully leave behind, and this new life, which I didn't yet feel fully a part of.

The deep emotional tension I felt in those early months wasn't just about missing home or struggling with language barriers— it was about the internal conflict of who I was becoming and who I had been. In my efforts to succeed and prove that I was worthy of the opportunities I had been given, I often neglected to acknowledge the emotional scars of leaving everything behind. The emotional journey toward independence wasn't just about becoming self-sufficient—it was about learning to reconcile the person I was with the person I was trying to become.

And yet, as the days turned into weeks and the weeks into months, I began to notice something changing within me. It was subtle at first—small, almost imperceptible shifts in my thinking and feeling. I began to realize that I wasn't just surviving; I was starting to live. I was beginning to see the possibility of a future that didn't feel so foreign and unattainable. The weight of my family's expectations, which had once felt like an unbearable burden, began to feel like a source of strength.

I wasn't just carrying the weight of their sacrifices—I was honoring them by doing everything I could to make this new life work. The pressure was still there, but I had begun to shape it into something positive, which drove me to keep moving forward and push through the uncertainty and the emotional turmoil. I wasn't doing it for them alone—I was doing it for myself.

Through the struggle, I learned that independence wasn't just about being alone—it was about finding strength within myself, even when I didn't feel strong. It was about embracing the challenges, the emotional highs and lows, and allowing them to shape me into the person I was meant to become. It wasn't easy. There were days when I felt completely lost, but there were also moments of clarity—small glimpses of the person I was becoming. And in those moments, I began to understand that the journey toward independence wasn't a linear path. It was messy, filled with contradictions, but it was mine, and that made it all the more meaningful.

The emotional journey toward independence was the most difficult part of my immigration experience, but it was also the most transformative. Looking back, I realize that it was in those quiet, lonely moments of doubt and fear that I was truly growing. I was no longer just the person who had left Iran with a suitcase full of hopes and dreams—I was becoming someone stronger, someone more capable, someone ready to face the challenges ahead.

In those early months, I had been on a journey toward independence, but it wasn't just about finding my way in a new country. It was about discovering who I truly was underneath all the layers of fear, doubt, and uncertainty. And it was in that discovery that I began to truly understand what it meant to be free.

The Struggle of Balancing Independence and Responsibility

One evening, after what felt like the longest day at work, I found myself sitting in the cozy living room of Shahla and Ray's home. The heater hummed softly, a quiet presence in the room, as I sat in the dim light, wrestling with the news I was about to share. I had found an apartment. The words felt like an achievement in my mind, a sign that I was finally taking control of my life. And yet, as I sat there, a part of me could hardly believe it. Was I ready? Could I truly make this leap?

I had spent days, even weeks, weighing the decision. I had barely started earning enough to support myself, and the thought of leaving the comfort and safety of Shahla and Ray's home filled me with a strange combination of excitement and dread. My heart raced with the need to prove to myself—and to them—that I was capable of moving on, yet my mind buzzed with the fear that I might be jumping into something I wasn't prepared for.

I rehearsed the words in my mind over and over, trying to sound confident, but every time I opened my mouth, the words felt fragile and tentative. I didn't want them to think I was just rushing into something. I wanted them to feel proud of me, to see that I was becoming independent, that I was ready to stand on my own. But beneath my calm exterior, a deep fear gnawed at me. I hadn't signed the lease yet. I hadn't figured out how I was going to make it work. I was still learning how to navigate this new life. And part of me feared they would see right through my façade.

When I finally blurted out the news, their response was everything I had hoped for. Shahla and Ray smiled, their pride in me radiating from their faces. Shahla hugged me, and Ray slapped me on the back, offering congratulations in his warm, fatherly way. But as they expressed their joy, a feeling of inadequacy crept into my chest, tightening with every word they said. The pride they showed felt so sincere, so genuine, but inside, I felt like an imposter. They were proud of the person I was trying to become, but I wasn't sure I was that person yet. How could I be ready for this? Was I making a huge mistake?

The weight of independence seemed to press down on me more with every congratulatory word, more with every step I took toward it. There was a part of me that longed to be the person they saw—a self-assured, capable man carving his path in a new world. But there was another part that still felt small, uncertain, lost.

That night, after the words had been spoken and the congratulations shared, I didn't return to the safety of their home. I couldn't. The reality of what I had decided began to sink in. Instead, I drove aimlessly, not sure where I was going, just needing to escape the suffocating weight of my own thoughts. Eventually, I parked my car by the bay, the city lights twinkling in the distance like a million tiny reminders of how far I still had to go. The ripples of the water reflected the storm inside me.

The silence was deafening. I sat there for hours, my mind a swirl of doubt and fear. Had I made the right decision? Was I truly capable of living alone, of making it on my own? Would

I find the strength to create the life I had always dreamed of, or was I simply deluding myself into thinking I could handle it? The questions wouldn't stop, each one more piercing than the last. The reality of the situation hit me like a tidal wave. This wasn't the romantic freedom I had envisioned. It wasn't glamorous or liberating. It was messy. It was uncomfortable. It was uncertain. And it was lonely.

For the next few nights, I found myself sleeping in my car by the bay. Every night, I would curl up in the backseat, trying to find some comfort in the cramped space, but there was none. My body ached from the uncomfortable position and the cold nipped at my skin, reminding me of just how far from home I truly was. The isolation pressed down on me, and I felt like an invisible presence in a world that didn't seem to care. Every morning, I woke disoriented, unsure of how to move forward. I felt as if I was waking up in a foreign country every time I opened my eyes.

The harsh reality of my situation—sleeping in my car, with no real home, no real foundation—hit hardest in the early hours, when the world was still, and all I could hear was the sound of my own heartbeat. There was no comfort, no security, no certainty. I had stepped into a world of independence, but it wasn't the freedom I had imagined. It was an unrelenting test. It was raw. It was painful.

And yet, there was something about it that stirred something deep within me—something I couldn't quite name. Yes, I was sleeping in my car, but I was doing it on my own. There was a strange, twisted pride in that. I wasn't relying on anyone else. I had made this decision, and no matter how difficult it was, I would see it through. Independence wasn't something given to you—it was something you earned, something you fought for. And this was my test. The difficulty of it, the loneliness, the uncertainty—it was all part of the process. It wasn't easy, but it was mine. It was a test of my resolve, of my ability to handle the pain of transition.

By the fourth day, I was exhausted. The weight of uncertainty, living out of my car, and struggling to find a sense of stability finally forced me to take action. I couldn't do it anymore—not like this. I needed something more. And so, I found an apartment, a modest space shared with two of my classmates. The idea of moving in with them brought a sense of relief I hadn't expected. It wasn't a victory that screamed of success, but it was a step forward. It was a roof over my head, a place I could call my own—even if it was shared. The apartment wasn't anything special—a small, unremarkable space—but to me, it felt like a sanctuary. A place where I could breathe without the crushing weight of uncertainty pressing down on me every moment.

In those first weeks in the apartment, I began to understand what it meant to balance independence and responsibility. Living with my roommates, I wasn't alone, but I was still responsible for myself. We shared meals, our dreams, our frustrations. We weren't just surviving—we were building something together, creating a small community in a foreign land. It wasn't the idealized version of independence I had imagined, but it was real. And that was enough for now.

Those early weeks were a test in themselves as I learned to balance the joy of small victories with the weight of responsibility. I wasn't just trying to survive—I was trying to thrive, to make my place in this strange new world. The apartment was a symbol of that. It wasn't glamorous, it wasn't easy, but it was mine. And that meant everything.

The Lingering Cultural Divide

As much as I wanted to settle into my new life, to embrace the American dream and the promise of a future full of opportunities, the reality of living between two worlds weighed heavily on me. At work, I could communicate just fine. The language was no longer an insurmountable barrier, but the nuances—the subtle rhythms and patterns that gave English its life—remained elusive. I could hold a conversation, yes, but there was always a lingering sense that I was missing something. It wasn't just the words; it was the unspoken undercurrents of the language—the jokes, the idioms, the familiar banter that seemed to flow so easily for others but always left me a step behind.

In meetings, people would laugh at jokes I didn't understand, and I would sit there, a smile frozen on my face, not out of politeness but out of sheer confusion. What did they mean? What was so funny? It wasn't just the humor; it was the rhythm of the conversation. The small talk, the casual references to pop culture or sports, the quick exchanges of personal stories—it all seemed like an ongoing puzzle that I was never quite able to solve. There was a constant dissonance, an ache in my chest, as if I were watching a play unfold but was never given the script.

It was an isolating feeling—being in a room full of people yet still feeling like an outsider. Sometimes, I would hear a joke or a reference that everyone else seemed to understand, and I would feel like I had missed a crucial lesson, as if I were always just a beat too late. How do you participate in a conversation when you don't know the rules? How do you engage in a culture when you don't yet know its language, not just the words but the very way people speak, the pauses, the gestures, the way humor is woven into every exchange?

This sense of being an outsider wasn't confined to work. Even in the simplest interactions, the casual moments on the street or in stores, I found myself lost. The American way of greeting people was different from what I was used to—more informal, more distant. I would walk into a store, and someone would say, "Hey, how's it going?" And for a moment, I would freeze. Was this a genuine question? Was I supposed to answer in detail, or just return a casual "Good, how about you?" Every encounter seemed to hold its own set of rules, its own expectations, and I never quite knew if I was playing by them. Every day felt like an endless guessing game, trying to figure out not just what people were saying, but what they meant by it.

And all the while, I carried the weight of my family's expectations. They had sent me here with dreams of success, of opportunity, and every time I stumbled, I felt like I was not only failing myself but also them. I didn't want to let them down. I wanted to prove that I could adapt, that I could succeed, that I could build a life worthy of their sacrifices. But every day brought new challenges, and the more I tried to fit in, the more I realized how far I still had to go.

It was Ray who saw the struggle beneath the surface. He could tell that I was frustrated, that I was battling something far deeper than the occasional language barrier. He saw how much I wanted to be part of this new world but also how difficult it was for me to truly feel at home in it. And while Shahla offered me the comfort of a familiar presence, it was Ray who pushed me to truly experience America, to dive headfirst into its culture, even if it meant making mistakes. He knew that learning a new language was just the beginning—that to really belong, I had to embrace every aspect of the culture, even the parts that felt foreign and awkward.

One night, after another awkward exchange at work, Ray noticed my frustration and decided to make a game of it. "Every time you make a mistake in English, you drop a quarter into the jar," he said with a smile. I didn't know whether to laugh or groan. The idea of intentionally making mistakes was foreign to me. I didn't want to mess up. I didn't want to be the one who stood out for the wrong reasons. But Ray's game wasn't just about language; it was about embracing the discomfort, the messiness, of learning. It was about accepting that I wasn't going to get it perfect—and that was okay.

At first, I was frustrated. I didn't want to be penalized for mistakes. Every quarter in the jar felt like a small weight on my shoulders. But as the weeks went on, I began to see it differently. Each coin was a reminder—a symbol of progress, of perseverance. The more quarters I dropped, the more I realized that each mistake was a step forward. The language wasn't just something I could master in isolation; it was something I had to live, something I had to breathe.

Ray also took it upon himself to introduce me to American football, a sport that, at first glance, seemed like an incomprehensible mess of rules, strategies, and jargon. The first time I watched a game with Ray, I could barely follow the plays, let alone understand what was going on. But Ray, with his characteristic patience, explained the basics, then moved on to the finer details. At first, I felt like a fish out of water, but slowly, I began to get it. The more I watched, the more I understood, and eventually, I wasn't just watching—I was invested. I started to root for the 49ers, to feel the pulse of the game. It wasn't just about the sport itself—it was about connecting to a part of American culture that had once felt so foreign to me.

But perhaps the most unforgettable moment of my cultural immersion came when Ray took me to the horse races. I had no idea how betting worked or what I was supposed to do, but Ray patiently guided me through the process. To my surprise, I won. Ray lost. We laughed about it, the kind of laughter that bridges gaps between cultures, between people who had once been strangers. In that moment, I realized that I wasn't just surviving in America—I was beginning to truly live here. The experiences I had once seen as foreign and confusing were now part of my reality. They were no longer just challenges to be overcome; they were the moments that defined my journey toward belonging.

Looking back, those seemingly small experiences became the building blocks of my understanding, the glue that began to hold me together as I navigated the complexities of living in a new country. They were the moments that, piece by piece, helped me bridge the gap between two worlds—my old one, and the new one I was trying to call home.

The Holidays: Joy and Longing

The holidays, particularly Christmas, became a complex emotional battlefield—a time of both joy and deep yearning. For the first time, I was immersed in the full force of American holiday cheer: bright lights, festive decorations, and the unrelenting cheer of carolers. It was unlike anything I had ever experienced in Iran. The streets shimmered with Christmas lights, like something out of a dream. The sheer abundance of it all—stores bursting with goods, homes decorated with lavish displays—was a spectacle that stirred something deep inside me. I was swept up in it, in the way people seemed to come alive with anticipation, as though the holidays were a universal bond that brought strangers together.

Shahla and I would go shopping together for small gifts for the few people we knew. We'd roam the aisles of department stores, picking out simple tokens of appreciation—nothing extravagant, but enough to capture the spirit of the season. As we walked through the bustling stores, the sound of cheerful Christmas music playing in the background, I could feel a small sense of belonging settle in my chest. It was as though I were becoming part of something larger than myself, something I could finally touch and take part in. It was new and exciting, and for brief moments, I could almost forget that I was far from home.

But no matter how much I tried to absorb the joy of the season, there was always an undercurrent of sadness that tugged at me. I couldn't escape it, even in the midst of all the newness. There were flashes of my family in Iran—my mother cooking the familiar dishes for the holiday meal, the sounds of my father's laughter filling the room, and the warm embrace of my siblings. I could almost hear the songs we sang around the table; the traditional prayers whispered in unison, the way our family would gather together in celebration. The sharp contrast between what I had left behind and what I was now experiencing in America was a bitter pill to swallow. It wasn't just nostalgia; it was a deep ache that seemed to grow stronger as the lights around me flickered with an artificial cheer.

I would find myself staring at the Christmas tree in Shahla and Ray's living room, the twinkling lights casting soft shadows on the walls, and I'd feel a knot tighten in my chest. It was beautiful, yes, but it was also a painful reminder of what I had lost. I was here in a world that wasn't mine, in a culture that was still unfamiliar, trying to carve out a new existence. But that deep longing for home—the smell of the food, the warmth of my family, the comfort of old traditions—never left me. Every gift I bought and every decoration I helped put up felt like a small betrayal of what I had left behind.

It was in the quiet moments, often in the evening after Shahla and Ray had gone to bed, that the sadness would take over. I'd sit by the window, watching the snow fall outside, and feel a deep sense of isolation. The world outside was celebrating, but I was mourning. The gap between the world I had known and the world I was trying to build was vast, and sometimes, it felt insurmountable. I longed for the old rhythms of the holidays— the gathering, the shared meals, the sense of family that was ingrained in every part of the celebration. In those moments, I realized just how much I had left behind in my journey to America. It wasn't just my family I missed; it was the way of life, the customs, the very essence of who I had been before this journey began.

There were parts of me—pieces of my identity, memories, traditions, ways of being—that could never be fully replicated in this new world. I couldn't bring the smells of my mother's cooking across an ocean, nor the sound of my father's voice in the stillness of the night. I couldn't recreate the warmth of our home, the laughter of my sibling filling the air. These were things I had to accept would be left behind. But even in that acceptance, there was a lingering grief. The holidays had always been a time of connection and unity, but now they felt like a painful reminder of the disconnection between where I was and where I had come from.

I knew that I had to learn how to honor those memories while moving forward. I had to figure out how to carry my past with me without letting it hold me back and how to navigate this new world while respecting the traditions that had shaped me. But it wasn't easy. Each holiday season felt like a test, a moment where the weight of everything I had left behind pressed down on me, asking me to choose between the world I had known and the world I was now living in.

As the Christmas season wore on, I began to realize that while the joy around me felt foreign, I had the ability to reshape it into something that could hold both my past and my present. I started to adopt small rituals—lighting candles at night, saying a prayer for my family, keeping a photo of them close. These small acts helped bridge the gap between the holidays I had left behind and the holidays I was now trying to create in this new land. They weren't the same, but they were mine. And that, in its own way, was enough.

The holiday season became a delicate dance of joy and longing, a time of celebration and reflection. It was a reminder that while the world around me might change, the love and memories I carried with me would always be a part of who I was. Even as I struggled to build a new life in America, those connections to my past—those bonds to my family and my homeland—remained strong, woven into the fabric of my new existence. The holidays weren't just a time of grief—they were also a time of growth, of learning how to carry my whole self into the future.

A New Understanding of Independence

As the weeks bled into months, and the months slowly accumulated into years, I found myself wrestling with a concept that had once seemed so simple—independence. At first, it felt like a straightforward thing: living alone, paying my bills, holding down a job. These were the markers of adulthood, the milestones that promised to prove I was capable of standing on my own two feet. I thought independence was simply about cutting ties from my past, making my own decisions and carving a path through this foreign land. But as time passed, I began to understand that true independence was far more complex and fragile than I had ever imagined.

It wasn't just about the external markers—the small apartment I could finally afford, the job that paid my rent, or the groceries I bought every week. Those things were necessary, of course, but they didn't define me. I soon realized that independence was about something deeper. It was about learning to trust myself when everything around me was uncertain, learning to face the unknown without succumbing to the paralyzing fear that had once gripped me at every new challenge. It was about becoming emotionally resilient, about acknowledging that I could be both strong and vulnerable at the same time.

For the first time, I had to confront the emotional side of independence—the loneliness that could creep in late at night when I was alone in my small apartment, the self-doubt that haunted me in quiet moments. The emotional weight of carrying everything on my shoulders began to settle in, and I found myself questioning my choices and the paths I had taken. Could I really handle this? Could I manage the responsibilities of my new life, or was I just one mistake away from losing everything? The fear was suffocating at times, a constant presence lurking in the back of my mind, always whispering that I wasn't enough, that I wasn't ready for this new life.

Yet, amid these quiet moments of self-doubt, I began to understand something profound: asking for help did not diminish me. It wasn't a weakness, as I had once feared; it was a form of strength, a way of acknowledging that I couldn't do everything alone. I grew up believing that independence meant never needing anyone, and that relying on others was a sign of failure. But in America, I learned that real strength came from recognizing that we are all interconnected and that even in my vulnerability, I could find power. Reaching out to friends for support and allowing myself to lean on others when the weight became too much to bear was not a betrayal of my independence—it was an embrace of it.

The people around me—Shahla, Ray, my roommates, and even colleagues at work—taught me this in subtle, unexpected ways. They didn't demand perfection from me. They didn't judge my mistakes or my missteps. They offered kindness, and in return, I offered my vulnerability. Slowly, I began to realize that this was a part of the process. Independence was not a solitary pursuit. It was a shared journey, a balancing act between standing firm on my own and allowing myself to be supported when I needed it. The beauty of it was that the more I allowed myself to be open, the more resilient I became. I wasn't building a life alone; I was building a life with others, learning to navigate the complexities of relationships and responsibilities in a new land.

In those early years, every day felt like an emotional rollercoaster. There were triumphs—moments when I felt proud of the strides I had made and caught myself handling a situation calmly and clearly. But there were also setbacks—moments when I stumbled, felt overwhelmed by the weight of expectations, and questioned if I was truly cut out for this new life. Yet, with every setback came a lesson. I learned that failure was not a reflection of who I was but a part of the journey I was on. It was through those failures that I found my greatest strength, my ability to rise again after each fall.

I began to understand that independence wasn't a destination. It wasn't something you achieved by ticking off a checklist of accomplishments. Independence was a journey, a process of continuous growth and transformation. And I was still on that journey, every step a new lesson in self-reliance and emotional strength. There would always be new challenges and new obstacles to overcome, but with each one, I grew a little stronger. I was learning not just how to survive in a new world but how to thrive in it—navigating its complexities, trusting myself in the face of uncertainty, and embracing both the joy and the struggle of independence.

Independence, I learned, was not about never needing anyone—it was about understanding that my strength came from within but also from the relationships I cultivated, the lessons I learned, and the resilience I built. It was about trusting that no matter how far I had come, I was never alone in my journey. And that, more than anything, became the cornerstone of my new life.

Chapter 7:
Matters of the Heart

When I first stepped foot in the U.S. and walked into that school, I felt a mixture of excitement and trepidation—a strange cocktail of emotions. I was eager to learn and adapt, but the vastness of it all left me dizzy. The world I had entered was as wide and intricate as a canvas I had never seen before. There were people from all corners of the globe—each with their own stories, their own experiences—and I was a stranger in all of it. But I quickly discovered that school, in all its overwhelming newness, was more than just an academic endeavor. It was a living, breathing microcosm of a much larger world, and it was within these walls that I would start to understand not only the people around me, but also myself.

It wasn't just about learning new subjects—it was about learning new emotions and new ways of connecting. Every day felt like a leap into uncharted territory, where new encounters, new faces, and new feelings were waiting to unfold. And the relationships I began to form—some fleeting, some lasting— became the threads that wove the fabric of my experience. It was through these connections that I learned what it meant to truly live in this foreign land. They weren't just moments of joy and discovery but also lessons in vulnerability, trust, and longing.

The first real bond I forged was with Ruth, a girl from Europe who, like me, had come to the United States to learn English. We were in the same ESL class, where the commonality of being outsiders brought us together. The conversations began simply enough—exchanging stories about our countries, our homes, and the strange new world around us—but there was an unspoken spark between us from the very beginning. Ruth's laughter was the first thing that drew me in. It was so pure, so spontaneous—like sunlight breaking through clouds on a gray day. Her joy was infectious, and her warmth was a refuge I didn't know I needed. In a world where I often felt like a stranger, Ruth made me feel seen. She had a way of listening that made me feel understood in a way I hadn't experienced in months.

Our friendship quickly blossomed into something deeper, though neither of us was prepared for it. There was no grand declaration, no sudden realization—we simply became a part of each other's lives in a way that felt natural. I remember one afternoon, during a casual conversation about food, I mentioned Persian cuisine, and Ruth's eyes lit up with curiosity. The way she leaned in, eager to hear more, touched me in a way I hadn't anticipated. She was genuinely interested, hungry not just for the food, but for the story behind it. I invited her to my apartment for dinner, and as she sat at my table, I explained the dishes with a quiet pride. Watching her reactions as she tasted my culture, her eyes wide with delight and surprise, was a moment of connection that transcended words. It wasn't just about food—it was about sharing a part of me, a part of my home that I had left behind. The laughter we shared over the kebabs, the rice, the unfamiliar flavors, marked the beginning of a deeper, more meaningful connection.

Over the next few months, Ruth and I became inseparable. We spent hours together—studying, talking, exploring this new world side by side. The world outside seemed to blur when we were together, as if time itself slowed down to allow us to savor each moment. There were nights when we would sneak into her room, close the door behind us, and talk for hours. These stolen moments were a refuge, a space where we could be raw and real with each other. We learned about our pasts, our dreams, our deepest fears. It wasn't always easy—language barriers and cultural misunderstandings cropped up, often leading to moments of confusion. But every misunderstanding was met with laughter, and every conversation left me feeling closer to her.

When Ruth had to return to her home country, the farewell was devastating. There were no grand promises of forever, no tears or dramatic farewells—but in the quiet space between us, I felt a deep emptiness. Saying goodbye to someone you've shared your soul with, even for a brief time, is never easy. The finality of it hit me with a weight I hadn't expected. Watching her leave, knowing that a chapter of my life was closing, was a silent grief. It wasn't just about the loss of Ruth—it was the loss of what we had built, of the possibility of what could have been. The weeks that followed were filled with a quiet, aching nostalgia. The simple act of remembering felt like a longing for something I could never quite reach again.

But life moved forward, as it always does. In time, I threw myself into my studies and work, trying to fill the void left by Ruth's departure with new distractions. It wasn't long before I met Françoise, another European girl who brought a spark of adventure into my life. Where Ruth had been steady and warm, Françoise was bold, spontaneous, a whirlwind of energy and enthusiasm. She had a way of making everything feel like an adventure—each moment with her was a new discovery. We would explore the city, take impromptu trips, and dive headfirst into experiences that left me breathless and alive. Françoise was a stark contrast to Ruth—but in her own way, she filled a different part of me. She was everything I admired—independent, free-spirited, and full of life.

But just as quickly as Françoise entered my life, she made the decision to leave. No explanation, no warning. I was blindsided. The suddenness of her departure left me feeling unmoored, as if the ground beneath me had shifted without any notice. I tried to understand, but she kept her reasons to herself. It wasn't until I spoke to one of her friends that I learned the truth—Françoise might be pregnant. The revelation hit me like a thunderclap. I cared for her deeply, and if it were true, I wanted to be there for her. I wanted to step up, face this challenge with her, and build something together. But by the time I arrived at the bus station to find her, she was already gone. Standing there, heart pounding, unanswered questions swirling in my mind, I felt like I had missed my chance. The sense of regret, of what could have been, haunted me for weeks.

In the aftermath, I couldn't help but reflect on what I had learned about myself at that moment. I had been willing to step up, to offer support without hesitation. I had been ready to take responsibility and show love and commitment, even without knowing what the future held. It was a turning point—a painful, bittersweet moment that reshaped my understanding of what it meant to love and be loved. I didn't get the answers I had hoped for, but I did get clarity. I understood, in the deepest parts of me, what it truly meant to care for someone, to be there for them, even when the future was uncertain.

As time passed, I met other people—other relationships that came and went, each leaving its mark on my heart. There was Katerina, the Brazilian girl whose vibrant energy and zest for life fascinated me. Then there was Sue, a warm-hearted South African whose kindness and empathy made her unforgettable. And Mahnaz—another Iranian girl who, despite the miles between us and the years that had passed, made me feel a little less like a stranger in this foreign land. But it wasn't just the relationships themselves that shaped me—it was the experiences they gave me, the opportunities for growth they provided.

And then, there was my work in the nightclubs—performing, surrounded by music, energy, and people from all walks of life. Each night on stage, I encountered new faces, new stories, and new ideas about love and connection. San Francisco, with its eclectic mix of cultures, was a place that offered endless opportunities to explore the intricacies of human emotion. And through these encounters—fleeting or lasting—I began to understand something profound: love is not just about romantic affection. It's about connection, about the moments when we are truly seen and understood. Love, in all its forms, transcends borders, languages, and cultures. It is the universal language of the heart.

These relationships—each unique, each profound in its own way—shaped my journey in ways I never expected. They taught me about vulnerability and how to truly connect with others. And in the end, they weren't just about the moments of love, but about the lessons they left behind—the lessons of self-discovery, of learning what I wanted from life and from love. Through all the laughter, the heartbreaks, and the goodbyes, I came to understand that love is, above all, a journey—a path full of twists, turns, and moments of clarity. It is the one thing that binds us all together, no matter where we come from or where we are going. And that, in itself, is one of the most beautiful discoveries of all.

Chapter 8:
Advice

It was Ray who first planted the idea in my mind: "Why don't you apply at Levi Strauss? It's a good company, steady work, and they treat their people well."

Levi Strauss & Co.—the name itself felt iconic, like a piece of America's history. In Iran, Levi's jeans symbolized freedom, of the West's modern, unrestrained spirit. Seeing someone wear Levi's meant they embraced something different—a world of opportunities and boundless ambition. And now, here I was, in America, being encouraged to join the very company that had represented so much more than just denim to me as a young man. The idea felt surreal, almost too ambitious. But Ray believed in me, and in that moment, I decided to believe in myself too.

With his help, I filled out the application. The forms were straightforward but felt like the first of many hurdles. My English, though improving, was still shaky, and I worried my limited vocabulary would betray my determination. When the call came inviting me for an interview, a cocktail of nerves and excitement churned within me.

Walking into the Levi Strauss headquarters, I felt a sense of awe. The air carried the faint scent of new fabrics, mingled with the hum of distant machinery. It felt like stepping into the heart of a giant. The interviewer, a middle-aged man with kind eyes and a calm demeanor, greeted me warmly. He asked about my background and my goals. I chose my words carefully, each one feeling like a small step across a tightrope. My voice trembled, but my determination shone through. Something in my earnestness must have struck a chord because, within days, I received the news: I was hired to work in the print room.

The morning I started, I walked through the factory doors with a mix of excitement and apprehension. The building buzzed with life. Machines clattered and whirred, their rhythms forming a backdrop to the murmur of voices. The print room itself was a vibrant world of its own, with rows of massive presses rolling out designs onto fabric. The smell of ink and cotton was intoxicating. To others, it might have seemed mundane, but to me, it was a gateway—a place where dreams began.

The work was repetitive, but I tackled each task with the zeal of someone who knew what was at stake. Every fabric I fed into the machines and every print I checked felt like another step forward. The monotony of the job didn't bother me; it was a symbol of stability in a life that had, until recently, been anything but stable. At the end of each week, holding my paycheck felt like holding proof that I belonged here, that I was building something meaningful.

But I didn't want to stay in the print room forever. A few months into the job, I overheard colleagues discussing a company program that helped employees further their education. My ears perked up. Could this be my chance to climb higher? I approached my supervisor hesitantly, asking for more information. To my surprise, he was supportive. "If you're serious about it, Levi's will back you," he said.

That night, I lay awake in my small apartment, staring at the ceiling, envisioning possibilities. The idea consumed me. I began researching local universities, eventually applying to Golden Gate University's evening program in marketing and advertising. The day I received my acceptance letter was unforgettable. I held the letter tightly, my vision blurring as tears welled in my eyes. For the first time, I felt I wasn't just surviving—I was thriving.

Balancing work and school was grueling. My days began early in the factory, where I managed the presses with precision. As soon as my shift ended, I would rush to university, often grabbing a quick bite to eat on the way. The lectures were fascinating but challenging. The language barrier made every lesson an uphill climb. My evenings stretched into late nights, pouring over textbooks, flipping through pages of unfamiliar terms, and practicing presentations in front of a mirror.

There were nights when exhaustion threatened to consume me. One evening, I found myself sitting at my kitchen table, my head resting on an open textbook, the clock ticking past midnight. The weight of fatigue pressed heavily on me, and doubts crept in. Why was I pushing myself so hard? Was it worth it? But then I thought of my parents back in Iran, of the sacrifices they had made to give me this chance. Their unwavering faith in me became my anchor, and I pressed on.

Despite the challenges, I began to excel. Marketing and advertising captivated me in ways I hadn't anticipated. I loved the creativity, the psychology, and the way it married art with strategy. Each class revealed another layer of my potential, and I felt like I was uncovering the person I was meant to become.

At work, my efforts didn't go unnoticed. A year after enrolling in school, I heard about an opening in the accounting department. It was a significant step up, and I was eager to prove myself. I applied, and when I received the promotion, I felt a wave of pride wash over me. Sitting at my new desk, surrounded by spreadsheets and financial reports, I realized how far I had come. I was no longer just a factory worker; I was contributing meaningfully to the company's success.

But life is rarely a straight path. After four years at Levi's, the company announced layoffs. When I received the news that I was among those being let go, the world seemed to tilt beneath my feet. The job wasn't just a source of income; it was a symbol of my journey, my progress. The uncertainty of what lay ahead felt suffocating, but I reminded myself of the obstacles I'd already overcome. If I had built myself up once, I could do it again.

****

My next venture was a surprising one: selling cars. The world of dealerships was fast-paced and cutthroat, a stark contrast to the structured environment of Levi's. At first, I struggled to find my footing. The art of negotiation, the psychology of sales—these were foreign concepts. But, I observed the veterans, learning how they built rapport and turned hesitation into trust. Slowly, I found my rhythm. Each sale became a small triumph, proof that I could adapt and succeed in unfamiliar territory.

Even as I found success in car sales, I knew it wasn't my ultimate calling. One day, while flipping through a newspaper,

I stumbled upon an ad for Farmers Insurance. They were seeking agents and offered a pathway to owning your own business. The idea ignited something within me. For years, I had worked to build others' dreams. Now, I wanted to build something of my own.

Becoming an insurance agent wasn't easy. The licensing exam was rigorous and filled with complex legal jargon that tested my resolve. I spent weeks immersed in study, often staying up late to memorize terms and concepts. When I finally passed the exam, the sense of accomplishment was overwhelming. For the first time in America, I was a business owner.

Running my own office was both exhilarating and challenging. I took pride in helping clients protect their homes, cars, and businesses. Each policy I sold felt like a step toward building a legacy, not just for myself but for the future I dreamed of. It was during this time that an unexpected opportunity arose: a chance to host a Farsi-language radio talk show.

The idea of connecting with the Iranian community in the Bay Area excited me. Hosting the show became one of the most rewarding experiences of my life. Each week, I spoke to listeners navigating the challenges of immigration, offering advice, sharing stories, and building a bridge between cultures. The show's success brought opportunities for advertising, and through it, I fostered deeper ties within the community.

One event I promoted was a concert for the renowned Iranian singer Morteza. Attending the concert that night, surrounded by the melodies of home and the energy of the crowd, I felt an indescribable connection to my roots. And in that sea of faces,

I met someone who would change my life forever. The encounter seemed serendipitous, a moment of clarity amidst the chaos of life.

Looking back, I realize that every challenge, every victory, had led me to that moment. Life is a series of connections, some planned, others unexpected. And often, the most profound moments are the ones we never see coming.

Chapter 9:
Night at Pasha

It was past midnight, and the energy of the night still coursed through my veins. My performance at the club had left me exhilarated, but not ready for the night to end. The streets outside were alive, buzzing with the hum of laughter spilling from doorways and the faint, hypnotic rhythm of distant music floating on the cool night breeze. Instead of heading home, I felt a pull toward something different, a yearning for a change of scene—and that's when Pasha came to mind.

I'd heard about Pasha, a Turkish-Arabic-style club, but had never experienced it for myself. The moment I stepped inside, I knew it was something special. The warm, amber lighting draped the space in a golden glow, flickering like candlelight. The air was perfumed with hints of exotic spices and incense, and the steady beat of the darbuka drums seemed to weave itself into my pulse. It was a world apart, a place where the ordinary melted away, leaving only the magic of the moment.

And then I saw her.

She sat at a table surrounded by people, but her presence outshone them all. Her laughter—soft, musical, and utterly enchanting—floated above the noise of the club, drawing me in like a melody I couldn't resist. The way she moved, the way her eyes sparkled as she spoke made everything else in the room blur into insignificance. I couldn't look away.

It wasn't the first time I'd felt attracted to someone, but this was different. Her presence stirred something deeper, something I couldn't quite put into words. For the first time in a long while, I felt unmoored, as though the ground beneath me had shifted.

Then, fate seemed to offer me a small gift—I recognized the man sitting beside her. An old friend from Iran. My pulse quickened. I made my way over to greet him; my focus split between catching up with him and stealing glances at her. She was talking to someone else, her smile lighting up her face, and I hesitated. How could I introduce myself without being too forward?

In a moment of nervous inspiration, I decided to leave my number with my friend, speaking just loud enough for her to hear. "Here's my number," I said, my voice slightly raised, hoping—praying—that she might remember it. But as the moments passed, I realized I couldn't just rely on chance.

I lingered a while longer, sipping my drink and watching her from across the room. I told myself it wasn't the right time, that the setting wasn't ideal. Yet, when I left the club, I carried her image with me. Her laughter replayed in my mind like a favorite tune, and her face haunted my thoughts in the most beautiful way.

For weeks, she remained an enigma. I had no name, no number, no way to find her, and yet she was all I could think about. Her laughter became a dream I couldn't shake.

And then came the concert in San Jose—a Morteza concert I'd been looking forward to for months. The crowd was vibrant, the air electric with anticipation as the first soulful notes filled the room. I was just settling into my seat, letting the music wash over me, when my gaze fell on her.

It felt like the world stopped.

There she was, just a few rows away, her profile illuminated by the dim glow of the stage lights. She was talking to a woman who looked so much like her they had to be sisters. My heart raced, torn between excitement and fear. This time, I couldn't let her slip away.

I made my way toward her, each step feeling like an eternity. "Hello," I said, my voice steady despite the storm of emotions inside me.

She turned, her eyes locking onto mine, and in that moment, I saw a flicker of recognition. "Hello," she replied, her smile as radiant as I remembered.

"You were at Pasha," I said, and her smile deepened.

"I was," she said. "You're friends with…"

And just like that, we were talking—easily, naturally, as though no time had passed. I asked for her name, eager to finally know the woman who had captivated me so completely.

"Zohreh," she said, and her name felt like poetry, soft and lyrical on my tongue.

We spoke about everything and nothing, the conversation flowing as if we'd been waiting our whole lives to find each other. Around us, the concert carried on, but it might as well have been a private performance for two. The music became the soundtrack to our connection, a steady rhythm underscoring the magic of the moment.

As the concert neared its end, I couldn't bear the thought of parting ways without seeing her again. "There's a party tomorrow at my friend's house," I said, hardly believing the words coming out of my mouth. "Would you like to come?"

She exchanged a glance with her sister before smiling. "I'd love to," she said, and with that, we exchanged numbers.

In the car ride home, I turned to my friend, my excitement spilling over. "I need a party tomorrow," I said, realizing I'd just made a promise I had no plan for.

He laughed, shaking his head. "You're unbelievable. Let's make it happen."

What followed was a flurry of phone calls and last-minute arrangements, but by the next evening, the party was ready. And when Zohreh arrived, it felt like the stars had aligned just for us.

From that night forward, our lives became entwined. Looking back, I see how every moment—every twist of fate—led me to her. It was as though the universe had been quietly orchestrating our story, weaving our paths together until we finally found each other.

Chapter 10:
Bad memory

During my college years, I juggled my studies with a late-night shift as a clerk at a gas station. It wasn't the most glamorous or fulfilling job—mostly quiet, monotonous, and steeped in solitude—but it provided a steady paycheck, which I desperately needed. Most nights, I passed the hours in a haze of routine, idly arranging items on shelves, keeping an eye on the clock, and occasionally chatting with the sparse stream of customers who wandered in. It wasn't exciting, but I never expected excitement. That was, until one fateful night turned my world upside down.

It started like any other shift. The fluorescent lights buzzed faintly overhead, casting a sterile glow across the small store. Outside, the gas pumps stood silent under the dim orange hue of the streetlights. The stillness of the night was broken only by the occasional hum of a car pulling in or the soft chime of the doorbell signaling a customer. I remember the clock ticking slowly, each minute dragging toward the end of my shift.

I was behind the counter, absentmindedly stacking candy bars, when the doorbell chimed again. I glanced up to see a man walk in, his movements deliberate but unhurried. He wore a dark hoodie, the hood pulled low over his face, obscuring his features. Something about him gave me pause—a strange tension in the way he moved, a certain weight to his presence—but I brushed it off. It wasn't unusual for late-night customers to seem tired or disheveled.

He approached the counter, and I greeted him with the usual, "Good evening. How can I help you?"

He didn't answer. Instead, he reached into his pocket and pulled out a gun.

"Give me all the cash!" he barked, his voice cold and sharp, cutting through the quiet like a blade.

For a moment, my mind went blank. The gun's barrel seemed enormous, its cold, dark metal gleaming under the fluorescent lights. My chest tightened as panic surged through me, and my heart pounded so violently it drowned out every other sound.

With trembling hands, I fumbled to open the cash register. My fingers felt clumsy, like they didn't belong to me. I grabbed the bills inside and handed them to him, my breaths coming in shallow gasps. Fear gripped me like a vice, squeezing tighter with each passing second. My mind raced, but there was no room for rational thought—only the instinct to survive.

But it wasn't enough.

"Open the safe!" he snapped, his eyes narrowing, the gun now pointed directly at my chest.

"I can't," I stammered, my voice barely above a whisper. "I don't have access to it. I swear."

"Don't lie to me!" he shouted, his frustration boiling over into rage. His hand trembled slightly as he tightened his grip on the gun, and I could feel the heat of his anger radiating toward me.

"I'm telling the truth!" I pleaded, my voice cracking. "I don't have the code."

He leaned closer, the gun now inches from my face. The tension was unbearable, the seconds stretching into an eternity. My mind screamed with the possibility of what might come next. Would he shoot me? Would I die here, in this cold, fluorescent-lit gas station?

Just then, salvation arrived in the form of tires crunching on the gravel outside. A car pulled up to the station, its headlights sweeping across the windows. The man froze, his eyes darting toward the door. For a brief moment, his focus shifted away from me. I held my breath, praying silently that whoever was in that car would come inside and scare him off.

After what felt like forever, he made a decision. Without a word, he turned and bolted for the door—but not before delivering a brutal parting shot.

The cold, hard metal of the gun's side struck the side of my head with a sickening thud. Pain exploded through my skull, and the world spun violently. My knees buckled, and everything went black.

When I came to, the harsh fluorescent lights stabbed at my eyes, and a chorus of voices swirled around me—urgent, concerned, unfamiliar. Blinking against the brightness, I saw the silhouettes of police officers standing nearby and the familiar figure of the gas station owner. One officer knelt beside me, his voice firm but kind.

"You're lucky," he said, his words cutting through the fog in my mind. "He didn't shoot you."

Lucky. The word echoed in my head, but I didn't feel lucky. My head throbbed, my body trembled, and the memory of the gun pointed at me was seared into my mind.

In the days that followed, I tried to return to normal, but normal no longer existed. Every noise, every shadow, every late-night customer felt like a potential threat. The gas station, once dull and uneventful, had become a place of dread. Though I eventually returned to my shifts, the weight of that night lingered, a constant reminder of how fragile life could be.

A couple of Sundays after the terrifying ordeal at the gas station, my good friend Ray suggested we go to the horse races. At first, I hesitated. The idea of spending a day at the racetrack felt foreign, almost frivolous, given everything I had been through. But Ray had a knack for persuasion, and with his usual charm, he convinced me that I needed a break.

"You've been through hell, my friend," he said, clapping a hand on my shoulder. "Come on, it'll be fun. You deserve a little excitement that doesn't involve dodging bullets."

He was right—I needed something to shake off the lingering weight of that night. So, with a mix of curiosity and reluctance, I agreed.

The moment we arrived at the racetrack; I was swept into a world unlike any I had ever known. The air was thick with anticipation and the scent of freshly cut grass. The grandstand teemed with energy—a kaleidoscope of people laughing, shouting, and cheering. Vendors called out, selling everything from hotdogs to programs listing the day's races. The rhythmic pounding of hooves echoed from the track, mingling with the occasional whinny of horses warming up.

Ray, a seasoned regular, moved through the bustling crowd with ease. "First time at the races, huh?" he teased, handing me a program. "Stick with me. I'll show you how it's done."

I followed him to the betting window, clutching the program like a lifeline. The names of the horses stared back at me, and I felt utterly clueless. Ray chuckled as he noticed my hesitation.

"Don't overthink it," he said. "Just pick a name that speaks to you. Trust your gut."

Scanning the list, my eyes landed on a name that struck me— *Golden Spirit*. Something about it resonated, though I couldn't explain why. "This one," I said, pointing.

Ray laughed. "Golden Spirit? Alright, rookie. Let's see how your beginner's luck holds up." He placed his own bets with the confidence of a man who had been doing this for years, grinning all the while.

When the race began, the atmosphere was electric. The announcer's voice boomed over the loudspeakers, calling the start. The gates flew open, and the horses surged forward like a tidal wave of raw power and speed. The crowd erupted in cheers, their voices a roaring symphony that matched the thunder of hooves on the track.

My heart pounded as I watched the horses streak past, their jockeys crouched low, urging them on. Dust kicked up from the track, shimmering in the sunlight. I gripped the edge of the railing, my eyes glued to the blur of color and motion.

To my astonishment, *Golden Spirit* pulled ahead in the final stretch. The cheers around me grew deafening as the horse surged across the finish line, its golden mane glinting like fire in the sunlight.

"I won!" I shouted, barely able to believe it.

Ray turned to me, his mouth hanging open in mock disbelief before breaking into laughter. "Unbelievable! Beginner's luck!" He clapped me on the back, shaking his head. "Here I am, the so-called expert, and I lose my bet, while you walk away with a win. You're going to be insufferable now, aren't you?"

We laughed all the way home, the exhilaration of the day still buzzing in my veins. When we arrived, Shahla was there to greet us, her warmth and hospitality an anchor after the chaos of the racetrack.

"You won? Really?" she asked, her eyes widening with surprise and delight.

"Yes, can you believe it?" I said, still grinning.

Shahla shook her head, laughing softly. "Well, that calls for a celebration." Without missing a beat, she headed to the kitchen, pulling out ingredients with practiced ease. The scent of saffron and roasted spices soon filled the air, wrapping the house in a comforting embrace.

As we sat around the dinner table, sharing stories from the day, the tension that had been weighing on me for weeks began to lift. Laughter echoed through the room, and for the first time in what felt like ages, I felt truly alive.

That night, as I lay in bed reflecting on the day, I realized something profound: life had a way of surprising me, even when I least expected it. Just when the shadows of fear and despair seemed too heavy to bear, the kindness of a friend, the thrill of a new experience, and the simple joy of a home-cooked meal reminded me that brighter moments were always within reach.

Chapter 11:
Heart Desire

After that magical party, Zohreh and I became inseparable. It was as though some invisible force had bound us together, threading our lives into a shared story that felt destined. Every moment we spent together deepened our connection, turning mere companionship into an all-encompassing love. Within three months, we made a decision that felt both thrilling and terrifying—we moved in together.

We found a modest apartment in Daly City, nestled just south of San Francisco. The building wasn't new, and the walls bore the marks of previous tenants, but it had a charm that made us feel at home. The windows faced the Pacific, and every evening, the fog would roll in like a silken veil, softening the world outside. That fog became a metaphor for us— mysterious, unyielding, and yet filled with infinite possibilities. Our apartment wasn't extravagant, but it was perfect. It was ours. Every corner held whispers of our laughter, and every morning felt like the beginning of something extraordinary.

Six months later, as naturally as the sun rising over the foggy horizon, we stood hand in hand, exchanging vows. The ceremony was simple—just a gathering of close friends and family—but it was as intimate and heartfelt as our love deserved. Zohreh looked breathtaking in her white dress, the fabric shimmering faintly in the soft light, but it was her eyes that stole my breath. They glistened with tears of joy, reflecting the life we were promising to share.

When she said, "I do," her voice wavered just enough for me to notice the depth of her emotion. My hands trembled slightly as I slipped the ring onto her finger. At that moment, it felt like the world had fallen away, leaving just the two of us standing on the precipice of forever. The cheers of our loved ones brought us back to reality, and as we kissed, sealing our vows, I realized this wasn't the culmination of our journey—it was the first chapter.

A year later, our love expanded in ways I couldn't have imagined. The day Zohreh gave birth to our son, the world seemed to stand still. I had never felt so helpless as I paced the sterile hospital hallway, waiting for news, but when the nurse finally brought me into the room, everything changed. Zohreh lay there, her face glowing with a mix of exhaustion and triumph, cradling a tiny bundle swaddled in soft blankets.

I held my son for the first time, his delicate fingers curling around mine with surprising strength, and I was overwhelmed. We named him *Kayvone* in Farsi, a name rich with heritage, and Kevin in English, a nod to the new world we were navigating. He was perfect—a piece of both of us and yet, entirely his own. Looking into his serene face, I felt an indescribable sense of purpose.

Life took on a beautiful rhythm after that. I worked during the day, and in the evenings, I returned to the warmth of our growing family. Zohreh would hum lullabies in Farsi as she rocked Kayvone to sleep, and I often found myself mesmerized by the sight of them together. Her voice was soothing, like a thread connecting our past to our present, and I knew I was witnessing something sacred. Our days were filled with small joys: laughter, shared meals, and whispered dreams of the future.

But life, as it always does, had more in store for us. One afternoon, my old friend Hoshiar called with a proposition that set our lives on a new course. "Come to Miami," he urged, his voice filled with enthusiasm. "We'll start a business together. There's an opportunity here, my friend. You'll see."

At first, the idea felt impossible. Miami was a world away from everything we had built in California. But the more we talked, the more the idea took root. Zohreh and I spent countless nights discussing the possibilities, her brow furrowed in concentration as we weighed the pros and cons. It was a difficult decision, but we agreed that if this move meant a better future for Kayvone, it was worth considering.

We decided to explore. Our journey began with a trip to Atlanta, where we stayed with one of Zohreh's family friends. Atlanta had its charm—the streets were lined with magnolias, and the Southern hospitality was undeniable—but it didn't feel like home. From there, we traveled to Miami, staying with Hoshiar and his family. Miami was like stepping into another world. The city pulsed with life, its vibrant colors and rhythms unlike anything we had known. The endless sunshine, the warm ocean breeze, and the multicultural energy were intoxicating.

One evening, as we walked along the beach, the waves lapping at our feet, I saw Zohreh's face light up. She looked out at the horizon, her hair tousled by the wind, and smiled—a smile that carried both hope and excitement. In that moment, I knew our decision was made. This was where our next chapter would unfold.

When we returned to Daly City, the real work began. We packed our belongings with a mix of excitement and nostalgia. Zohreh, ever practical, carefully wrapped our keepsakes, her hands lingering over photo frames and small treasures that held memories of our early days. Each item told a story, and as we boxed them up, it felt like we were saying goodbye to one life while preparing to embrace another.

The day of the move was bittersweet. Zohreh and Kayvone flew to Miami ahead of me, their journey quick and easy compared to what lay ahead for me. I rented a U-Haul trailer, loaded it with everything we owned, and hooked it up to my white Ford LTD. As I prepared to leave, Zohreh stood on the porch, holding our son. Her eyes were filled with love, tinged with just enough worry to tug at my heart.

"Drive safely," she said softly, her voice catching.

"I will," I promised, kissing her gently. "I'll see you soon."

As I pulled away, the familiar streets of Daly City disappeared in the rearview mirror. The fog that had become a symbol of our life there gave way to the open road. The journey to Miami was grueling, stretching on for days, but it was also exhilarating. With every mile, I felt the weight of our decision and the promise of what lay ahead.

By the time I reached Miami, my heart was racing with anticipation. When I pulled into the driveway of our new home, Zohreh was waiting at the door, holding Kayvone. Her face broke into a radiant smile as I stepped out of the car, and in that moment, every hardship, every mile, was worth it. I wrapped my arms around them, holding tight to the two people who had become my entire world.

Together, we were ready to face whatever the future held. It didn't matter where we lived or what challenges came our way—our love and the life we had built together was more than enough to see us through.

The journey to Miami stretched over eight grueling days, each one a test of my endurance, patience, and resolve. The vast stretches of highway seemed to stretch endlessly, the horizon always just out of reach. I set a steady pace, driving for eight hours each day before pulling over to rest, letting the engine cool and my mind find moments of stillness. Yet, solitude was a double-edged sword—peaceful in some moments, crushing in others. The quiet hum of the road offered ample time for reflection, a bittersweet mix of nostalgia for what I was leaving behind in Daly City and the uncertainty of the new life awaiting me in Miami.

About halfway through my journey, I reached Texas, where my old friend Bijan lived with his wife, Zahra, and their newborn son, Pejman. Their home was a beacon of warmth, a temporary sanctuary from the isolation of the road. When I arrived, Bijan greeted me with a bear hug, his laughter filling the air as he clapped me on the back. "You look like a man who's been living on gas station coffee and stale sandwiches," he joked, his grin infectious.

Zahra, equally welcoming, ushered me inside, where the rich, familiar aroma of Persian spices enveloped me like a comforting embrace. She was in the kitchen, her hands deftly working on a feast fit for royalty. "You're too thin," she said, wagging a wooden spoon at me. "Tonight, we're going to fix that."

As Zahra prepared dinner, Bijan's eyes twinkled with mischief. "Go grab your Tombak from the trailer," he said, leaning against the doorway with his arms crossed. "Let's see if you've still got it."

Bijan had always been a musical prodigy, his talent unmatched by anyone I'd ever met. The thought of playing alongside him again filled me with a mix of excitement and nervous anticipation. I retrieved my Tombak from the trailer, the case slightly scuffed from the journey but still protecting the memories it held.

We started to play—tentatively at first—but soon, the music flowed as if no time had passed. Bijan's fingers moved effortlessly across the strings, his melodies weaving through the air like magic. The room came alive with sound; each note a bridge to the past, a reminder of simpler times when our biggest worries were hitting the right chords. Laughter punctuated the music as we stumbled through old favorites, our spirits lifted by the shared joy of creation.

That night, as we sat down to dinner, Zahra's cooking transported me straight back to Iran. The flavors were rich and familiar, each bite a reminder of home. We talked late into the evening, sharing stories, dreams, and laughter, the kind that comes from being with people who truly know you.

The next morning, after a hearty breakfast and heartfelt goodbyes, I thanked Bijan and Zahra for their hospitality before resuming my journey. The Texas sun rose high in the sky as I drove away, their warmth lingering like an ember in my chest.

But the road ahead was not without its challenges.

By the time I reached Mobile, Alabama, I felt the strain of the journey settling deep into my bones. My car's fuel gauge dipped precariously close to empty, and I had no choice but to pull off the freeway in search of a gas station. The small, weathered station I found was bathed in the orange glow of a fading sunset, its neon sign flickering weakly as if struggling to stay alive.

As I stepped out to fill up the tank, a sense of unease prickled at the edges of my awareness. The air felt heavier here, charged with something I couldn't quite name. I tried to focus on the task at hand, but my eyes were drawn to the side mirror of my car.

A group of men stood nearby, their postures tense, their clothes worn and dusty. They looked like they had just stepped off a construction site, but their eyes weren't on their work—they were on me. Their low murmurs carried across the lot, their glances sharp and cutting.

My heart began to race. I knew what this was. The hostage crisis in Iran had inflamed anti-Iranian sentiment across the United States, and I was suddenly, painfully aware of how vulnerable I was—a lone traveler in an unfamiliar place, marked by the features of my heritage.

One of the men, a burly figure with a baseball bat slung over his shoulder, tapped the bat against his palm as he whispered something to the others. They laughed—a sound that carried no humor, only menace. My throat tightened as they started to move toward me, their steps deliberate, their expressions dark.

Every instinct screamed at me to run.

I fumbled with the gas pump, my hands trembling as adrenaline surged through my veins. Dropping the nozzle, I bolted for the driver's seat, slamming the door shut and locking it in one fluid motion. My hands shook as I turned the key in the ignition, the engine sputtering to life just as the men reached my car.

"Hey!" one of them shouted, slamming a fist against the hood.

I didn't wait to see what would happen next. Throwing the car into gear, I peeled out of the gas station, gravel flying in my wake. My tires screeched as I sped down the road, the men's angry shouts fading into the distance.

In my rearview mirror, I saw them give chase on foot, their forms growing smaller with each passing second. Relief mixed with fear as I realized they had given up, retreating back to the shadows of the gas station.

But the encounter left me shaken. My hands gripped the steering wheel tightly as I merged back onto the freeway, my mind racing with what-ifs. How quickly strangers had judged me, their anger fueled by headlines and misplaced blame. I wasn't the enemy, but to them, I was a stand-in for their rage— a convenient target for a world they couldn't control.

The road ahead stretched out endlessly, but now it felt heavier, burdened by the weight of that moment. Still, I reminded myself of why I was doing this. I thought of Zohreh's smile and Kayvone's tiny hands reaching for mine. They were my light in the darkness, the reason I kept going.

By the time I reached Miami, the memory of Mobile still lingered, a stark reminder of the challenges that came with living between two worlds. But when I saw Zohreh standing at the door of our new home, holding our son in her arms, her face breaking into a radiant smile, the weight lifted.

Together, we had taken a leap into the unknown, and no matter what lay ahead, I knew we would face it side by side.

Chapter 12:
Moving

When I finally arrived in Miami, every muscle in my body ached from the eight-day journey. The miles of endless road stretched behind me like a lifeline and a chain—binding me to the choices I had made, yet propelling me forward toward an uncertain future. Zohreh and Kayvone were staying with Hoshiar, his wife, and her mother-in-law. Their modest home, filled with chatter and the scent of freshly brewed tea, was a stark contrast to the lonely hum of my car and the isolation of the open highway.

The moment I stepped through the door, Zohreh's smile met me like a beacon. She had a way of grounding me, even when the world felt like it was spinning out of control. Kayvone toddled toward me with outstretched arms, his laughter the sweetest sound I had heard in weeks. I scooped him up, burying my face in his hair. In that instant, the exhaustion, the doubts, and the ache of leaving everything behind melted away.

For the next few days, we stayed with Hoshiar's family, grateful for their kindness. Their home, though small and crowded, was alive with the kind of warmth only family could provide. Zohreh and I spent the evenings quietly discussing our next steps while Kayvone played in the corner, blissfully unaware of the challenges his parents were trying to navigate.

It didn't take long to find a rental house near their neighborhood. It was far from perfect—peeling paint clung stubbornly to the walls, and the lawn was a mix of stubborn weeds and dry patches. But it was ours. As we moved in, Zohreh took charge, unpacking with a determination that seemed almost defiant, as if daring the universe to challenge her resolve. I watched her arrange the kitchen, her movements precise and deliberate, and I felt a wave of gratitude. She wasn't just making a home—she was building the foundation of our new life.

For my part, I tried to focus on what had brought us here in the first place: the business. Hoshiar had always been the dreamer, his words brimming with enthusiasm and his eyes lit with possibilities. It was his vision that had convinced me to take this leap, to leave behind the familiarity of Daly City for the unknown of Miami. Now, it was time to turn those dreams into something real.

One evening, we decided to visit him at the pizza restaurant where he worked while attending college. The moment we walked in, the warm, savory aroma of fresh dough and bubbling cheese enveloped us. The restaurant was alive with the sounds of clinking plates and cheerful chatter. Behind the counter, I spotted Hoshiar. He moved with an effortless grace, tossing pizza dough high into the air before catching it with a practiced spin.

When he noticed us, his flour-dusted face broke into a wide grin. "Just give me a few minutes," he called over the din. "I'll make something special for you!"

We found a table near the back and waited as he worked his magic. True to his word, he brought out a pizza so large it could barely fit on the table. It was loaded with every topping imaginable, a masterpiece of indulgence. As we ate, savoring each bite, the restaurant began to quiet down. Finally, Hoshiar joined us, sliding into the booth with a weary but triumphant smile.

"This is amazing," Zohreh said, holding out a slice for him to try. "You'll have to teach me your secrets."

He laughed, shaking his head. "The secret is a lot of practice—and a little bit of luck."

As the conversation shifted to the business, I felt a surge of anticipation. This was the moment we had been working toward, the reason we had uprooted our lives. I leaned forward, my voice steady but eager. "So, Hoshiar, let's talk about the partnership. Zohreh and I have been saving for this. We're ready to invest. What's the plan?"

For a moment, his expression remained neutral, but then I saw it—a flicker of hesitation, a shadow crossing his face. He glanced down at the table, avoiding my gaze.

"I've been meaning to talk to you about that," he said, his voice quieter now. "I don't have the money to invest. Things have been... tighter than I expected."

His words landed like a blow, each syllable a weight pressing down on my chest.

I stared at him, struggling to process what I had just heard. "Wait, what?" I asked, my voice sharp. "If you don't have the money, why did you tell me to come here? Why make it sound like everything was ready to go?"

He shrugged, offering a sheepish smile that only deepened my frustration. "I thought maybe things would work out," he said, his tone almost casual, as if this wasn't the foundation of my family's entire future.

Anger rose in me, hot and uncontrollable. This wasn't just a misunderstanding—this was a betrayal. Zohreh's hand found mine under the table, a gentle squeeze that pleaded for calm, but I couldn't hold back entirely.

"You *thought* things would work out?" I repeated, my voice trembling. "Do you have any idea what we gave up to come here? The risks we took? You didn't just waste my time—you uprooted our lives!"

He had no answer, only an apologetic look that did little to soothe the fire burning in my chest. For a moment, I considered pushing further, demanding answers, but then I saw something in his expression—a weariness, a quiet desperation. This wasn't malice; it was recklessness, the kind of blind optimism that collapses under the weight of reality.

I leaned back, exhaling deeply as the disappointment settled over me. The move, the dream, the promises—it all felt like a mistake.

Zohreh broke the tension with a soft laugh, though it didn't quite reach her eyes. "Well," she said, lifting Kayvone from his high chair, "it looks like we'll have to figure out something else. Right?"

Her resilience was a reminder of why I had fallen in love with her. Even in the face of uncertainty, she found a way to move forward.

That night, as we drove back to our rental house, the city lights casting shadows across the dashboard, I couldn't shake the feeling of regret. Miami, with its vibrant energy and endless sunshine, suddenly felt cold and uninviting. But as I glanced at Zohreh, her eyes fixed lovingly on our sleeping son, I reminded myself of the real reason we had come.

This wasn't just about starting a business. It was about giving my family a chance at a better future, no matter how uncertain the road ahead might be. The path had taken an unexpected turn, but together, we would find a way forward.

After deciding to move on from the disappointment of the failed business plans in Miami, I poured my energy into finding a stable job. It wasn't just about supporting my family—it was about rebuilding my sense of purpose and regaining the confidence I'd lost along the way. After several interviews and plenty of persistence, I landed a position as a salesman at a Nissan auto dealership. The work was fast-paced, competitive, and, at times, overwhelming, but it was exactly what I needed. Every car I sold felt like a small victory, a reminder that I could navigate this new chapter and carve out a path for us.

One morning, during a busy shift, the phone rang at my desk. It was my turn to answer. Straightening my tie, I picked up the receiver and spoke in my best professional tone: "Nissan of Miami, this is [your name]. How can I assist you today?"

A confident, melodic voice greeted me on the other end. "Hi, I'm interested in a Nissan Z sports car. Do you have any in stock?"

"Yes, absolutely," I replied, my enthusiasm genuine. The Nissan Z wasn't just a car—it was a statement, a sleek, high-performance machine that turned heads wherever it went. "It's a fantastic car. When would you like to come in for a test drive?"

There was a brief pause before she responded. "How about tomorrow? Around 11 a.m.?"

"That works perfectly," I said, jotting down the appointment in my logbook. "We'll have it ready for you. Looking forward to meeting you."

The next day, I arrived early, determined to make a good impression. I handpicked one of our most stunning Nissan Z models—a metallic silver beauty that gleamed under the Florida sun. As I gave it a final polish, I felt a mix of excitement and nerves. It wasn't every day that someone called specifically for a car like this. Whoever she was, she had great taste.

At precisely 11 a.m., she arrived. She walked through the dealership doors with an air of confidence, her movements deliberate and self-assured. Her attire was elegant yet understated, and her presence immediately drew attention. She introduced herself with a warm smile, and I couldn't help but feel a surge of eagerness to impress her.

After browsing the lot, she pointed to the car I had prepared. "That one," she said, her eyes gleaming with anticipation. "Let's take it for a spin."

Grabbing the dealer plate—a magnetic one we used to cover the license plate during test drives—I fixed it securely to the back of the car. As I opened the driver's side door, she stopped me.

"You drive first," she said, her voice smooth and casual. "I want to see how it handles before I get behind the wheel."

It wasn't an unusual request. Many customers preferred to observe before taking over, so I slid into the driver's seat without hesitation. As I started the engine, the car roared to life, its powerful motor humming like a beast ready to be unleashed. I guided it through our usual test-drive route, highlighting the car's features and capabilities. She listened intently, nodding at my explanations and asking insightful questions. It was clear she knew exactly what she wanted.

After a few blocks, she leaned back and said, "Okay, I'm ready to drive now."

I pulled over and parked, stepping out of the car and expecting her to do the same. The heat of the midday sun pressed down on me as I adjusted my tie, waiting for her to join me. But instead of opening her door, she slid into the driver's seat, closed the door, and—with a quick glance in the rearview mirror—slammed her foot on the gas pedal.

The tires screeched as the car shot forward, leaving me standing there in stunned disbelief. The Nissan Z roared down the street, its silver body gleaming as it disappeared around the corner.

For a moment, I was frozen, unable to process what had just happened. My mind raced with questions. Had I misread her intentions? Was this really happening? The only thing in my hand was the magnetic dealer plate I had removed moments before. It was as though she had vanished, taking not just the car but my composure with her.

The reality of the situation hit me like a wave, and the heat of the day suddenly felt unbearable. Drenched in sweat, my suit clinging uncomfortably to my skin, I realized I had no cell phone to call for help. This was before mobile phones were common, so my only option was to find a payphone.

I began walking, my polished dress shoes clicking against the pavement as I scanned the area for a phone booth. Each step felt heavier than the last, my frustration mounting with every block. Finally, I spotted a payphone and rushed to it, fumbling for change. My hands trembled as I dialed 911.

"911, what's your emergency?" the operator asked, her tone calm and professional.

"A woman just stole a car from our dealership during a test drive," I blurted out, giving them all the details I could remember—the make and model, her description, and the direction she had gone. After filing the report, I called the dealership.

"It's me," I said when my manager picked up. "The woman who came in for the test drive—she took off with the car."

There was a pause before he spoke. "Are you okay?"

"I'm fine," I replied, though my pride was anything but intact.

"Stay where you are," he said, his tone reassuring. "We'll send someone to pick you up. Don't worry about it—we'll handle this."

Back at the dealership, my manager met me with a firm pat on the shoulder. "These things happen," he said, his voice steady. "Honestly, she probably needed the car for something shady. We'll report it to the insurance company, and the police will find it in a few days."

His calm demeanor was a relief, but I couldn't shake the humiliation. The memory of her driving off, leaving me stranded and bewildered, played on a loop in my mind. As I got into my own car to head home, exhaustion settled over me like a heavy blanket.

When I pulled into the driveway, Zohreh was waiting on the porch, holding Kayvone. Her smile was like a beacon, chasing away the shadows of the day. As I embraced her and our son, the weight of the incident began to lift. In the face of setbacks and challenges, I reminded myself of what truly mattered: my family, my resilience, and the unwavering determination to keep moving forward.

Chapter 13:
Disappointment

The weeks following the stolen car incident at the dealership were among the most trying times I'd experienced since moving to Miami. Each morning, I'd wake up with a sense of unease—a mix of lingering disappointment from our failed business plans and the stark reality that my job was little more than a stopgap. My dreams of thriving in Florida had unraveled faster than I could have imagined.

Late one afternoon, as I drove home from another grueling day at the dealership, a knot of worry coiled tighter in my stomach. I couldn't help but question every decision that had led us here. Would things have been different if we had stayed in California? Had I dragged my family across the country for nothing?

When I finally pulled into the driveway of our modest rental home, I stepped out into the warm Miami evening, the humidity clinging to my skin like a second layer. As I walked up to the front door, I realized the house was oddly quiet. Usually, Kayvone's laughter or the muffled sound of music would greet me. Instead, I found Zohreh standing in the hallway, her face lit with a warm smile that instantly made my heart feel lighter.

Her eyes sparkled with a quiet excitement. She cradled our son, her other hand resting gently on her belly in a way that felt more deliberate than usual.

"What's going on?" I asked, slipping off my shoes. A small spark of hope flickered in my mind—maybe she had cooked my favorite dish or planned a surprise to lift my spirits.

Zohreh took a slow breath, her smile widening. "I have news," she said, her voice soft yet brimming with barely contained joy. "We're going to have another baby."

In that single moment, all the strain and frustration of the past months evaporated. It was as if every worry melted into the background, drowned out by the sound of my own pounding heart. My jaw dropped, and a tremor of emotion rippled through me.

"Really?" I managed to say, stepping closer so I could cradle both her and Kayvone in my arms. The significance of this moment was overwhelming. In one breath, our little family of three was about to grow, our love about to expand in a way that made every setback seem inconsequential.

"Yes," she said, tears of happiness edging her eyes. "We're going to be a family of four."

For a moment, we just stood there—locked in an embrace that felt more like coming home than any house could ever provide. Kayvone wriggled in her arms, peering up at us with innocent curiosity, as if sensing he was no longer going to be an only child.

That night, we sat at the kitchen table long after Kayvone had fallen asleep, talking about our future. But our conversations felt different—lighter, more hopeful. We were no longer just navigating disappointment; we were planning for a new life that demanded more stability, more certainty. Suddenly, the idea of returning to California took on a new urgency.

We reflected on the reasons we had moved to Florida: the business plan with Hoshiar, the promise of opportunity, and a fresh start. But the reality had been far from what we'd hoped. Now, with a second child on the way, every decision mattered even more. We needed the support of old friends, the familiarity of the place we once called home, and the sense of belonging we'd left behind.

"Yes," I admitted quietly, meeting Zohreh's gaze across the table. "I think it's time to go back."

Her relief was palpable. Though we had both tiptoed around the topic, neither of us wanted to admit our Florida plans had faltered so drastically. But with the news of the baby, our priorities crystallized. We could no longer afford to wait for a business that might never materialize or endure jobs that felt more like placeholders than genuine opportunities.

Over the next days and weeks, our conversations turned into tangible plans. We began researching neighborhoods in California, calling old friends to see if anyone had leads on jobs or housing. The spark of excitement we had lost in Florida rekindled as we scoured online listings and reminisced about the places we loved back West. Each step felt like part of a greater design—a return to the roots that would support our growing family.

The nights, meanwhile, were filled with whispered dreams. We would lie in bed, Zohreh's head on my shoulder, talking softly about how we wanted our children to grow up surrounded by people who truly understood us, who spoke our language and shared our traditions. We imagined Kayvone playing with the new baby in a safe backyard, in a neighborhood where we felt welcome. We thought about weekend get-togethers with friends who were like family, and the comfort of being in a place that no longer felt foreign.

Day by day, the decision to leave Miami for California took shape. We gathered boxes once again, packing up the remnants of a chapter that hadn't gone as planned but had nonetheless taught us the value of resilience and the strength of our bond. Yes, we had faced disappointment and uncertainty, but this news of our second child was a beacon reminding us that our story was far from over. In fact, it was just beginning.

Finally, the day of departure arrived. Standing in the now-empty living room, I surveyed the packed boxes and the bare walls that had once held our hopes for a better life in Florida. Zohreh stood beside me, her hand resting gently on her still-flat stomach, the promise of new life shimmering in her eyes. Kayvone clutched at her leg, sensing the shift in our world but too young to understand its significance.

****

Leaving Miami felt like stepping off a stage in the middle of a performance—abrupt, tinged with regret, yet somehow inevitable. On our last morning in the city, the humidity clung to the air as if it refused to let us go. I woke up before dawn, disturbed by a restless energy I couldn't quite name. As the first slivers of sunlight crept through the blinds, I listened to the faint sounds of the city: distant car horns, the rustle of palm trees, and the hum of life already stirring in a place that had never truly become home.

Our modest rental house was nearly empty. The once cozy living room, where Zohreh and I had shared countless late-night discussions about our failing business plans, now stood barren. Boxes lined the hallway, half of them already shipped off or given away. The walls, once bearing pictures and reminders of our short-lived Florida chapter, were stripped bare, echoing the hollowness I felt inside. The only signs of life were the remnants of our last hurried breakfast—a couple of plates and a single mug I hadn't packed yet.

Zohreh was in the bedroom, folding the final set of clothes into a suitcase. Despite the uncertainty weighing on us, she moved with a calm determination. She had always been the more resilient one, facing life's turns with grace. Her pregnant belly was just beginning to show, a gentle curve that reminded us of how our family was growing, how we were about to welcome another life into our midst. Every time I caught sight of her profile, my heart clenched with a mixture of protectiveness and guilt. I had promised her stability here, and instead, we were leaving behind dashed dreams and unfulfilled promises.

Outside, the Miami heat was already intensifying, promising a scorching afternoon. I loaded our final suitcases into the trunk, the sweat beading on my forehead. With each item I placed inside, I felt the weight of the decision to leave piling up. My mind flickered through all the memories—both good and bad—that we had forged in Florida: the bright spark of hope when we first arrived, the slow erosion of that hope when our business plan crumbled, the stolen Nissan Z incident at the dealership that left me feeling humiliated and disillusioned. The more I recalled, the more certain I became that it was time to move on.

By the time we locked the front door for the last time, I felt an odd mix of sadness and relief. I stood there for a moment, my hand on the doorknob, as if expecting some part of Miami to call me back or grant me closure. But nothing came—just silence and the rustle of a stray palm frond in the light breeze. Zohreh, holding our son Kayvone's tiny hand, offered me a sympathetic smile, and that was all the encouragement I needed to walk away. We climbed into the car, the engine sputtering to life in the humid morning air, and drove off.

The highway to the airport was unusually quiet, as though the city itself was still waking up and had no time to bid us farewell. "I never thought it would end like this," I murmured, breaking the silence. Zohreh placed her hand gently over mine on the gearshift, squeezing it in a gesture of understanding. We didn't need words to acknowledge the whirlwind of thoughts and emotions passing between us. Our eyes, when they met, spoke volumes about the mixture of disappointment and optimism we shared.

Arriving at the airport, we navigated the maze of departures, the overhead signs a blur of directions to gates leading to countless destinies. We hauled our luggage to the check-in counter—Zohreh wincing slightly at the exertion, protective of the life growing inside her. Kayvone clung to her leg, his young mind oblivious to the magnitude of what was happening. For him, it was just another adventure, an airplane ride that would take him someplace new.

At the gate, we settled into plastic chairs among fellow travelers—each lost in their own story of endings and beginnings. Outside the enormous windows, we could see planes taxiing in the bright Florida sun. The smell of engine fuel and recycled air filled the terminal, a scent that spoke of transitions and journeys yet to unfold.

As we boarded, the narrow aisles of the plane only magnified the sense of leaving something behind. We stowed our carry-ons overhead, strapped ourselves in, and waited for the engines to roar to life. When the plane finally lifted off, I looked out the window at Miami's skyline receding into the distance, the blue of the Atlantic glimmering under the sun. My throat tightened. This was the end of a dream we had chased so eagerly not long ago.

Yet, when I turned to look at Zohreh, gently rubbing her belly, and at Kayvone, wide-eyed with excitement, hope stirred within me. We might be leaving behind broken aspirations in Miami, but we were carrying forward the most precious things of all—our family, our resolve, and a second child whose future depended on us taking this leap back to California. I reached for Zohreh's hand, intertwining our fingers as the plane banked to the west, signaling our journey toward the unknown future that lay ahead.

In that moment, I realized that sometimes, the bravest decision is to step away from a life that isn't working, no matter how much we once believed in it. We had come to Florida with ambition, but we left with something more profound—a deeper understanding of our resilience and a renewed appreciation for the bond that held us together. It wasn't the life we expected, but it was a stepping stone to the life that awaited us back in California.

And as the plane soared higher, breaking through the cloud cover, I felt a surge of determination. If we could weather the disappointments of Miami, we could face whatever challenges might come our way. In each other and in our growing family, we had the foundation we needed to build a new future—one full of promise, love, and the unshakeable faith that, this time, things would be different.

Chapter 14:
Going Back

The moment our plane touched down at San Francisco International Airport, an overwhelming sense of relief and joy washed over me. It was as if the city itself greeted us with open arms, welcoming us back to a place that felt more like home than any we'd known in Florida. The crisp Bay Area air and the faint whiff of the ocean were an instant reminder of why we'd left California in the first place—but also why we had returned. Dreams might have led us away, but love and resilience had brought us back.

After gathering our luggage, we headed to the car rental desk. My heart fluttered with anticipation as we navigated the busy terminal. Lines were long, and the travelers around us had their own stories of departures and arrivals, but it felt like we were the only ones in the world on a new beginning. A cheerful clerk handed us the keys to a modest sedan, and we stepped out into the bright sunlight, the car glinting as we loaded our bags.

The drive toward our old apartment complex was a journey of rediscovery. The highways, the exit signs, even the traffic itself carried a familiarity that made my chest ache with gratitude. The rolling hills around San Francisco, the skyline punctuated by skyscrapers, and the distant silhouette of the Golden Gate Bridge made me feel like I was flipping through the pages of a cherished photo album. Each turn on the freeway was a reminder that we were no longer in the land of unfulfilled promises—this was a new start in a place that understood us, and that we understood in return.

Our spirits soared as we pulled up to the apartment complex. It looked just as we remembered: a row of units with ivy climbing the walls and a small courtyard where neighbors gathered on warm evenings. The manager, a kindly older woman, greeted us with a broad smile. "Welcome back," she said, her voice warm with nostalgia. "Feels like you never left." Those words were balm to our weary souls. We signed the final paperwork, took the keys, and headed up to our old unit—a place that, despite its modesty, felt infused with memories and new possibilities.

Inside, the apartment was empty, echoing every sound we made. The starkness of the rooms could have been unsettling, but I felt an electric current of happiness, a feeling that we'd come home. Zohreh and I set our suitcases in the bedroom, and little Kayvone squealed with excitement as his footsteps echoed on the bare floors. The emptiness was a promise that soon, this space would be filled with the warmth of our family and the belongings that made our life ours.

The next few days were a whirlwind of anticipation. Our furniture and other belongings were still en route from Florida, somewhere on a truck slowly making its way across the country. The waiting was both thrilling and maddening. We slept on borrowed air mattresses, used plastic utensils and paper plates for meals, and hung our clothes on makeshift racks. Yet, the sparseness didn't dampen our spirits. Each morning, I woke up to see the sun filtering through the windows, illuminating the promise of a fresh start. The air was still cooler than Miami's humid climate, a gentle reminder that we were back in the Bay.

Meanwhile, as we settled in, we couldn't ignore the fact that Zohreh's belly was gently rounding—a quiet celebration that never left our thoughts. She moved through each day with a grace that left me in awe, carrying our second child and radiating a serenity that told me everything would be alright. Even in our half-furnished apartment, her presence filled the emptiness with a glow of impending life.

Zohreh's prenatal visits at the local clinic reassured us that everything was on track. The doctor's gentle smiles and the heartbeat we heard on the ultrasound were moments that brought tears to my eyes. Each new sign of our baby's health felt like a miracle. Some evenings, we would lie on our temporary bedding, and I'd rest my hand on her belly, feeling the baby's tiny kicks. In those moments, surrounded by cardboard boxes and the promise of our furniture's arrival, we laughed at how life had turned so unexpectedly—and yet felt so right.

At last, the call came: our moving truck would arrive that afternoon. The tension in my chest unraveled as I saw the massive truck rumbling up the street. Its arrival felt like a grand parade, even if it was just a couple of movers in worn uniforms. They swung open the back hatch, and there it all was—our couch, our dining table, our memories. Box by box, they carried pieces of our history into our old apartment that now glowed with the spirit of a fresh beginning.

As we unwrapped each item, Zohreh would show Kayvone the plates, the trinkets, and the books, explaining their significance as if rediscovering them herself. We found small treasures—a favorite mug, a lamp that had once been a wedding present—and each one triggered a cascade of fond recollections. The apartment transformed from an echo chamber of possibilities into a living space threaded with love and continuity. By the time we set up the living room and placed our bed in the bedroom, it was like we had never left. The air mattress, the plastic plates, and the emptiness were replaced by the comforting sight of our life in tangible form.

That evening, we collapsed onto the couch, exhausted but elated. I glanced over at Zohreh, who rested her hand on her belly. The baby gave a small kick as if in approval. With Kayvone in my lap, eyes drooping from the day's excitement, I felt the most profound sense of contentment. We were home—truly, undeniably home.

In the days that followed, I quickly found work at a local dealership. Each sale, each handshake, felt like a step toward stability, a testament to our resilience. And through it all, the gentle reminder of new life continued to bloom in Zohreh's growing belly. Every flurry of motion in her womb was a reminder of why we were here, why the trials of Miami had been worth enduring: because sometimes you need to lose a bit of yourself to understand where you truly belong.

Finally, as her due date approached, we found ourselves discussing baby names and preparing Kayvone for the role of an older sibling. There were late-night conversations about the future, endless rummaging through baby clothes, and tender moments where we felt our unborn child kicking in response to my voice. It was a quiet, powerful joy—knowing that we were welcoming a new member into a family that had already braved so much.

On the day of her scheduled delivery, we woke before dawn. The city was still, the fog rolling in over the rooftops in soft waves. There was a quiet tension in the air, a mix of excitement, nerves, and a profound sense of wonder at what lay ahead. We kissed Kayvone goodbye, leaving him in the loving care of Shahla and Ray, and drove to the hospital. The ride felt surreal, and each traffic light was a reminder of how ordinary life continued while ours was about to change forever.

At the hospital, nurses guided us through the maze of corridors, their smiles reassuring. The operating room was bright and methodical, a flurry of measured activity. Standing by Zohreh's side as the anesthesiologist prepared her, I could see both fear and resolve in her eyes. I held her hand tightly, whispering words of comfort and gratitude. After a short while, I heard the first cries of our second child—an echo of pure life and possibility.

They placed our newborn son into Zohreh's arms for a moment before carefully swaddling him. We named him Kayhan, a name that symbolized the expanse of the universe and the vastness of our love. In that moment, time seemed to slow, the room fading into a blur of clinical lights and hushed voices. All that mattered was the tiny life in front of us and the family we had become.

As we left the hospital days later, the car seat fitted snugly in the backseat; it struck me how different this experience felt compared to our life in Miami. We were home, surrounded by familiar streets and the promise of the life we had once envisioned. Yes, there were still challenges. We hadn't magically solved every issue, nor had we regained every dream that Miami had once represented. But in the hush of that drive back to our old/new apartment, with Kayhan murmuring softly. Zohreh leaning her head on my shoulder, I realized that sometimes the greatest leaps forward come not from chasing something entirely new but from returning to where you started—wiser, stronger, and ready to grow with whatever life brings next.

Chapter 15:
That's Life

Not long after we brought home our second child, it became painfully clear that our modest apartment was no match for a growing family of four. Baby toys cluttered the living room, and half-folded laundry seemed to appear in every corner. The cozy space we had once cherished now felt stifling. Late one evening, as Zohreh and I tried to navigate through a sea of baby gear and boxes of diapers, we locked eyes, each of us sharing the same unspoken realization: *We can't stay here much longer.* Despite the relief of having found stability in San Francisco, the cramped quarters and our children's needs demanded change.

I began crunching the numbers, researching apartments that might offer more space—but with every calculation, the city's skyrocketing rent cast a daunting shadow over our plans. Time after time, I came to the same conclusion: *If we're going to pay that kind of rent, we might as well buy.* The notion of purchasing a home both thrilled and frightened me. I had no idea how to tackle a down payment, let alone navigate the labyrinth of mortgages. Yet, whenever my doubts grew too loud, I pictured Kayvone and Kayhan racing through a backyard of their own, and it reminded me why the risk was worth it.

In desperation and determination, I turned to Ray, who helped me regain a foothold at Levi Strauss & Co. Walking back into the building felt like recovering a piece of my identity—a reminder of the confidence I once carried. But as the first few paychecks came in, I realized that a standard nine-to-five alone wouldn't magically accumulate the down payment we needed. So I dove into any side gig I could find. My afternoons became devoted to drum lessons, sharing my lifelong passion with eager students whose enthusiasm fueled me just as much as the extra income. On top of that, I still performed at a nightclub a few nights each week—an exhilarating, late-night affair that left me both energized and exhausted.

Still, even with those extra earnings, I was falling short. That's when an overnight position at Avis Rent a Car presented itself. Before I knew it, my schedule had transformed into a near-impossible jigsaw puzzle:

- **7:00 AM to 3:00 PM:** Levi's, where I clung to steady employment.

- **4:00 PM to 6:00 PM:** Drum lessons, teaching bright-eyed students.

- **6:30 PM to 9:00 PM:** A rushed, precious window of sleep.

- **9:30 PM to 1:00 AM:** Nightclub performances, my passion for music helping to pay the bills.

- **1:00 AM to 6:00 AM:** Overnight shift at Avis, fielding exhausted customers and last-minute rentals.

- **6:00 AM to 7:00 AM:** Rush home for a quick shower, then off to Levi's, the cycle repeating itself.

For six grueling months, I lived in a fog of near-constant exhaustion. Sometimes I'd doze off in the break room at Levi's, head propped on a table, heart pounding at the thought of missing my next shift. Other days, I'd nap in my car, lulled by the steady hum of the engine. The fatigue was a constant companion, but so was the image of Zohreh balancing our newborn while corralling a curious toddler. Whenever I felt like quitting, that image reminded me of my purpose: to secure a real home, a place where our children could thrive.

Slowly but surely, my bank account began to reflect the fruits of this relentless schedule. Every dollar I earned went straight into savings—no frills, no indulgences. Memories of Ray's refusal to co-sign still stung my pride, but in a way, it galvanized me. I became determined to prove I could do it on my own—no safety nets, no handouts, just hard work and unwavering resolve.

Then came the house hunt—a venture that tested my patience almost as much as my overnight shifts had tested my endurance. My first modest condo attempt fell through when the loan officer murmured an apologetic refusal. "I'm sorry," he'd said, sliding the papers back to me. "You simply don't qualify." Each rejection felt like a personal failure, yet it also reignited my determination. If it took another six months of sleepless nights, so be it.

One weekend, I stumbled upon a real estate agent who seemed to share my grit. She'd call me excitedly about new listings, determined to find something that wouldn't crush my budget. Week after week, I juggled showings with my rotating shifts, sometimes ducking out of Avis the moment my shift ended, the sun barely peeking over the horizon as I drove to meet her. After countless disappointments and close calls, we finally found a modest house in Concord—a far cry from the sky-high prices in the city. It was older, the paint peeling in spots, and the yard needed attention, but the layout had potential. My children would have enough space to play, and the neighborhood seemed calm and family-friendly.

Negotiations began, and the process felt like a high-wire act. The agent worked magic I didn't know existed, finding creative financing solutions that let us inch toward the necessary down payment. Even then, my heart pounded every time I heard a phone ring, fearing more rejection. Finally, one afternoon in the realtor's office, the papers were laid out in front of me. I signed on the dotted line, surrounded by the scent of stale coffee and the creak of office chairs. My hands trembled with a mix of triumph and disbelief, realizing that with each signature, I was climbing a mountain I once thought insurmountable.

Moving day arrived in a rush of cardboard boxes and swirling emotions. The house stood empty, an echoing shell waiting for our laughter and our life. Zohreh, her belly slightly rounded with our second child, held Kayvone's hand as we stepped through the front door. We took in the worn carpet, the chipped paint, and the echo of our voices in the bare living room, and I felt a surge of gratitude so strong it nearly brought tears to my eyes. We were homeowners—no co-signer, no shortcuts, just pure determination and faith.

In that living room, I paused to reflect on how we'd gotten here: the failed business in Miami, the stolen car at the Nissan dealership, and the grueling schedule of multiple jobs. Yet, here we were, stronger for every trial. This house was more than four walls—it was a testament to how far we'd go to give our children a future.

That night, after we'd lugged in the last box and Kayvone and Kayhan were finally asleep, Zohreh and I sat on the floor of our living room, our voices echoing off the empty walls. We talked about paint colors and furniture arrangements, but mostly, we spoke about the life we envisioned here—family dinners, birthdays, holidays, and quiet evenings spent reading to the kids. Outside, the Concord night was peaceful, the sky awash with stars that hinted at endless possibilities.

I took Zohreh's hand in mine, remembering how she'd endured each setback with unflinching support, how her presence had been the compass guiding me through every dark moment. The walls might need work, the yard might be overgrown, but in that moment, the house glowed with the warmth of everything we'd overcome. As exhaustion tugged at my eyelids, I closed my eyes and breathed in the promise of a new beginning. Yes, the road had been arduous, but every mile of it had led us here—to a place we could truly call home.

End of Volume 1